Our Best
Family Recipes

No-stress recipes for family meals, holiday celebrations, church suppers & more!

D1565574

To everyone who loves cooking for family & friends!

Gooseberry Patch
From our Kitchen to Yours

Gooseberry Patch
An imprint of Globe Pequot
246 Goose Lane
Guilford, CT 06437

www.gooseberrypatch.com
1 800 854 6673

Copyright 2020, Gooseberry Patch
978-1-62093-403-6

••••••••••••••••••••

Do you have a tried & true recipe... tip, craft or memory that you'd like to see featured in a **Gooseberry Patch** cookbook? Visit our website at www.gooseberrypatch.com and follow the easy steps to submit your favorite family recipe.

Or send them to us at:
Gooseberry Patch
PO Box 812
Columbus, OH 43216-0812

Don't forget to include the number of servings your recipe makes, plus your name, address, phone number and email address. If we select your recipe, your name will appear right along with it... and you'll receive a FREE copy of the book!

CONTENTS

Easy
Family-Favorite
Recipes

::::::::::::::::::::::

Our Best Family Recipes

We all love getting together with family & friends, whether it's for Sunday brunch, football Friday night or a big holiday meal. Sometimes planning for a get-together can be daunting, so we've gathered some of our handiest tips for serving up delicious dishes without a lot of fuss.

- Many recipes are scaled for 4 to 6 servings, but can be easily doubled. For soups and stews, double or triple all the ingredients, except for the liquid, seasonings, cornstarch and herbs.

- Use your trusty slow cooker to serve casseroles, appetizers and even desserts. Best of all, it keeps food at the right temperature.

- Consider setting out dishes buffet-style. It's an easy way for guests to serve themselves.

- Make space at your table by using cake stands and stacking multi-height serving platters for rolls, breads, appetizers, sandwiches and desserts.

- Try making mini versions of your favorite dishes, such as individual size meatloaves, quiches, pot pies or desserts. Muffin tins make this fun and easy!

- Don't be afraid to buy pre-washed and pre-cut veggies. It's a great way to save time for soups, salads, casseroles and side dishes.

- Pasta dishes are a great way to save a few pennies.

- Let everyone pitch in! People love to help, and by letting everyone bring their favorite side dish, salads or desserts, you'll spend less time in the kitchen and have more time to enjoy their company!

Scrumptious Stuffed Potato Skins, Page 28

CHAPTER ONE

Appetizers

Parmesan Zucchini Sticks, Page 18

Baked Spinach & Artichoke Dip, Page 34

Lisa Johnson, Hallsville, TX

Ranch Ham & Tortilla Pinwheels

These are a favorite of all ages...after school, after work or just because!

Makes 3 dozen

1 c. deli smoked ham, cubed
2 8-oz. pkgs. cream cheese, softened
0.4-oz. pkg. ranch salad dressing mix
2 green onions, minced
14 12-inch flour tortillas
4-oz. can diced green chiles
Optional: 2-1/4 oz. can sliced black olives, drained

Mix together ham, cream cheese, ranch dressing mix and green onions in a bowl; spread on tortillas. Sprinkle with chiles and olives, if desired. Roll tortillas tightly. Chill 2 hours or up to 24 hours. Slice rolls into one-inch pieces.

Jenni Shoaf, Woodland Hills, CA

Cucumber Bites

For a fancy finish in a snap, spoon cheese spread into a pastry bag fitted with a large star tip. Swirl onto cucumber rounds.

Makes 2 to 3 dozen

2 cucumbers
5.2-oz. container cream cheese spread with garlic & herbs
Garnish: thinly sliced smoked salmon, minced hard-boiled egg yolk, snipped fresh dill

Remove thin strips of peel from cucumbers with a potato peeler; slice 1/2-inch thick. Top each slice with one teaspoon cheese spread; garnish as desired. May be covered and chilled up to 3 hours before serving time.

★ DOUBLE DUTY ★ Easy edible relish dish! Slice just a bit from the bottom of a cucumber lengthwise so it will stand. Then, slice off the top third, scoop out the seeds and fill with olives and pickles.

Ranch Ham & Tortilla Pinwheels

Kathy Harris, Valley Center, KS

Brown Sugar Fruit Dip

Delicious any time of year, but especially during the holidays.

Serves 8 to 10

8-oz. pkg. cream cheese, softened
1/2 c. brown sugar, packed
1 c. sour cream
1 t. vanilla extract
1 c. frozen whipped topping, thawed
gingersnap cookies or assorted fruit slices

In a bowl, beat cream cheese and brown sugar with an electric mixer at medium speed. Add sour cream and vanilla; beat until blended and smooth. Fold in whipped topping. Cover and chill for at least 4 hours before serving. Serve with gingersnaps or fruit.

Barbara Parham Hyde, Manchester, TN

Stuffed Strawberries

Try using pecans in place of the walnuts for added variety.

Makes 18

20 strawberries, hulled and divided
8-oz. pkg. cream cheese, softened
1/4 c. walnuts, finely chopped
1 T. powdered sugar
Optional: fresh mint leaves

Dice 2 strawberries; set aside. Cut a thin layer from the stem end of the remaining strawberries, forming a base. Starting at opposite end of strawberry, slice into 4 wedges, being careful not to slice through the base; set aside. Beat remaining ingredients together until fluffy; fold in diced strawberries. Spoon 1-1/2 tablespoonfuls into the center of each strawberry. Refrigerate until ready to serve. Garnish with fresh mint leaves, if desired.

★ HOT TIP ★ For an edible, glittery garnish to brighten up appetizer trays... roll grapes, strawberries and blueberries in extra-fine sugar. Festive AND delicious!

Brown Sugar Fruit Dip

Gail Konschak, Millville, NJ

Marinated Shrimp Appetizer

A flavorful appetizer that's simple to prepare for a special gathering.

Serves 8 to 10

2 onions, thinly sliced
1-1/2 c. oil
1-1/2 c. white vinegar
1/2 c. sugar
1/4 c. capers, undrained
1-1/2 t. celery seed
1-1/2 t. salt
2 lbs. medium shrimp, cooked
  and peeled

Combine all ingredients except shrimp in a large bowl; mix well. Add shrimp; stir to coat well. Cover and refrigerate for 6 hours or up to 24 hours, stirring occasionally. Drain shrimp, discarding the marinade.

★ SAVORY SECRET ★ It's best to let frozen shrimp thaw overnight in the fridge, but if you're in a hurry, place the frozen shrimp in a colander and run ice-cold water over it. Don't thaw shrimp in the microwave, as it will get mushy.

Jo Ann, Gooseberry Patch

Sherried Shrimp Sandwiches

These little gems are a party favorite in our family!

Makes 56

1-1/2 lbs. uncooked small shrimp
3-oz. pkg. shrimp, crawfish and crab
  boil
4-oz. pkg. crumbled blue cheese,
  softened
1/2 c. cream cheese, softened
Optional: 1/4 c. sherry
5 green onions, minced
1/2 c. celery, diced
1/2 c. walnuts, finely chopped and
  toasted
1/2 t. seasoned salt
1/4 t. cayenne pepper
112 slices party pumpernickel bread
Garnish: fresh dill sprigs

Cook shrimp using seafood boil according to package directions; drain. Peel shrimp and devein, if desired. Chop shrimp. Stir together shrimp and remaining ingredients except bread and garnish. Spread about one tablespoon filling on each of 56 bread slices. Top each with another bread slice. Cut sandwiches in half diagonally. Garnish, if desired. Store sandwiches covered with a damp paper towel in an airtight container in refrigerator.

Marinated Shrimp Appetizer

Penny Caldwell, Bristol, TN

Couldn't-Be-Easier Tapenade

We love olives at our house, so I decided to try to come up with an olive tapenade recipe using the inexpensive black and pimento-stuffed green olives I always have on hand. The result was a hit! We often serve it over grilled chicken too.

Makes 12 servings

6-oz. can black olives, drained
1 c. green olives with pimentos
1 clove garlic
3 T. olive oil
3 T. balsamic vinegar
1/2 t. salt
Optional: 1/2 c. fresh parsley, chopped
1 loaf French bread, sliced and toasted, or pita chips

In a food processor, combine all ingredients except bread slices or chips. Pulse lightly to desired spreading or dipping consistency. To serve, spread on toasted bread slices or scoop up with pita chips.

Donna Anderson, McHenry, IL

Texas Cowboy Caviar

Add a few diced jalapeños for a little heat if you like!

Makes 15 servings

16-oz. can black-eyed peas, drained and rinsed
16-oz. can pinto beans, drained and rinsed
16-oz. can black beans, drained and rinsed
15-oz. can shoepeg corn, drained
1 onion, chopped
1 c. celery, chopped
1 c. green pepper, chopped
Optional: 4-oz. jar pimentos, drained
1 c. oil
1 c. vinegar
1 c. sugar
corn chips

Combine beans, corn, onion, celery, pepper and pimentos, if desired, in a serving bowl. Whisk together oil, vinegar and sugar in a saucepan and heat to a boil. Cook until thickened. Remove from heat; cool to room temperature. Drizzle oil mixture over vegetable mixture and toss to mix. Cover and refrigerate at least one hour to overnight; drain excess liquid before serving. Serve with corn chips.

Couldn't-Be-Easier Tapenade

Patti Harris, Hendersonville, TN

Cheese & Beef Dip in a Bread Bowl

After discovering this yummy appetizer at a teacher luncheon, I've shared it with family at a number of get-togethers. Always a welcome treat!

Makes 20 servings

1 round loaf French, Italian or
   Hawaiian bread
2 8-oz. pkgs. cream cheese, softened
16-oz. container sour cream
1.35-oz. pkg. onion soup mix, or
   less to taste
4-oz. pkg. sliced pressed beef or
   ham, chopped
1/2 c. celery, chopped
1/2 c. black olives, chopped

Cut off top of bread loaf. Tear top into chunks; pull chunks out of inside of bread to create a bowl effect. If desired, toast chunks in the oven to make dipping easier. Cover and set aside. In a bowl, mix together remaining ingredients. Dip may appear thin at first, but will set up. Spoon mixture into bread bowl. Cover and chill for at least one hour to allow flavors to blend and the dip to set. Serve with bread chunks.

Jackie McBride, Barnesville, OH

Mom's Tasty Kielbasa

My mom made this for my wedding reception...she's had the recipe so long that her copy is faded. It has a sweet-and-sour taste that's so delicious!

Serves 8 to 10

1 c. onion, sliced
1 c. celery, chopped
1 to 2 T. butter
1/2 c. catsup
1 t. Worcestershire sauce
1/4 c. vinegar
1/4 c. sugar
1 T. mustard
1 t. paprika
1 lb. Kielbasa, sliced into 1-inch pieces

In a skillet over medium heat, sauté onion and celery in butter until tender. Add remaining ingredients except Kielbasa. Mix well; add Kielbasa and bring to a boil. Reduce heat; simmer until sauce thickens, stirring often.

★ SAVVY SWAP ★ If you don't happen to have a round loaf of bread handy, serve dips and salsas in hollowed-out sweet peppers, artichokes or tomato halves...no bowls to wash!

Cheese & Beef Dip in a Bread Bowl

Marion Sundberg, Ramona, CA

Parmesan Zucchini Sticks

Serve these tasty zucchini sticks instead of French fries alongside cheeseburgers...kids will gobble them up!

Makes 4 servings

1 egg
1/2 c. Italian-flavored dry bread crumbs
1/2 c. grated Parmesan cheese
1 t. dried thyme
1/2 t. pepper
6 small zucchini, quartered lengthwise
Garnish: ranch salad dressing

Place egg in a shallow bowl and beat well; set aside. Mix bread crumbs, cheese, thyme and pepper in a separate bowl. Dip zucchini pieces into egg and then into bread crumb mixture; place on a lightly greased baking sheet. Bake at 450 degrees for 20 to 25 minutes, until tender. Serve with ranch salad dressing for dipping.

Amy Butcher, Columbus, GA

Parmesan-Artichoke Crostini

I took the familiar (and popular) artichoke dip, jazzed it up with chopped green chiles and red peppers, then spread it over baguette slices. Save time by looking for toasted baguette slices in the supermarket bakery or substitute bagel chips or Melba toast rounds.

Makes 3-1/2 dozen

1 baguette
12-oz. jar marinated artichoke hearts, drained and chopped
4-1/2 oz. can chopped green chiles, drained
1 c. mayonnaise
1 c. grated Parmesan cheese
1/4 c. red pepper, finely chopped
2 cloves garlic, minced

Diagonally cut baguette into 42 1/4-inch thick slices. Reserve any remaining baguette for other uses. Arrange slices on large ungreased baking sheets. Broil slices one to 2 minutes or until toasted. Stir together chopped artichoke hearts and remaining ingredients. Spread one tablespoon artichoke mixture on toasted side of each baguette slice. Bake at 450 degrees for 6 to 7 minutes or until lightly golden and bubbly.

Parmesan Zucchini Sticks

Vickie, Gooseberry Patch

Smoky Chicken Spread

This savory, crunchy spread is always a hit at parties.

Makes 10 to 12 servings

3 c. cooked chicken, finely chopped
1/2 c. celery, finely chopped
1/2 c. smoked almonds, coarsely
   chopped
1/4 c. onion, finely chopped
3/4 c. mayonnaise
1 T. honey
1/2 t. seasoned salt
1/8 t. pepper
assorted snack crackers

In a bowl, combine all ingredients except crackers; mix well. Cover and chill at least 2 hours before serving. Serve with snack crackers.

Vickie Garlitz, Edmond, OK

Working Moms' Cheese Ball

This is easy, quick and tasty! Use whatever flavor of cream cheese you have in the fridge...dill, garlic, onion and chive are all tasty.

Makes one cheese ball

2 8-oz. containers flavored
   spreadable cream cheese
1/2 to 1 c. mixed shredded cheese
1/2 to 3/4 c. finely chopped pecans
Optional: hot pepper sauce to taste

Blend cream cheese and shredded cheese in a medium bowl; add hot pepper sauce, if desired. Form into a ball; roll in chopped pecans. Wrap in plastic wrap and refrigerate for an hour before serving.

★ HANDY TIP ★ **Toasting really brings out the flavor of chopped nuts... and it's simple to do. Add nuts to a small dry skillet. Cook and stir over low heat for a few minutes, until toasty and golden.**

Smoky Chicken Spread

Naomi Townsend, Ozark, MO

Green Chile Sourdough Bites

We like to serve these tasty appetizers when our car club friends gather after a car show. I like to use small loaves of sourdough bread.

Makes 12 servings

4-oz. can diced mild green chiles
1/2 c. butter, room temperature
1/2 c. mayonnaise
8-oz. pkg. shredded Monterey
    Jack cheese
1 loaf sourdough bread, cut into
    small bites
garlic powder to taste

In a bowl, mix chiles, butter and mayonnaise until smooth. Add cheese and stir to combine. Mixture may now be covered and refrigerated for later use. Spread chile mixture onto bread pieces. Arrange in a single layer on an aluminum foil-lined baking sheet. Sprinkle with garlic powder. Bake at 450 degrees until bubbly and crisp, about 3 to 4 minutes.

Karen Boehme, Greensburg, PA

Karen's Cayenne Pretzels

These spicy-hot pretzels are always a hit!

Makes 8 to 10 cups

1 c. oil
1-oz. pkg. ranch salad dressing mix
1 t. garlic salt
1-1/2 t. cayenne pepper
2 10 -oz. pkgs. pretzel twists

Mix together first 4 ingredients; pour over pretzels in a large bowl. Stir until well coated; spread onto ungreased baking sheets. Bake at 200 degrees for one hour and 15 minutes to 1-1/2 hours.

★ GREAT GIFT ★ A snack-attack basket is a perfect gift for college students! Fill a colorful basket with Karen's Cayenne Pretzels, mixed nuts, chocolate-covered pretzels, potato chips and easy-to-make jar mixes!

Green Chile Sourdough Bites

Athena Colegrove, Big Spring, TX

Homemade Guacamole

The buttery flavor of ripe avocados makes guacamole my favorite comfort food...I could eat the whole bowl by myself!

Serves 6 to 8

6 avocados, pitted and peeled
2 to 4 cloves garlic, minced
1 lime, halved and divided
1 tomato, diced
1/2 onion, diced
salt to taste
Optional: 1 diced jalapeño pepper, chopped fresh cilantro
tortilla chips

Combine avocados, garlic and juice of 1/2 lime in a large bowl; mash to desired consistency. Gently stir in tomato, onion, salt and juice of remaining 1/2 lime; add jalapeño and cilantro, if using. Cover and chill for 30 minutes to one hour; stir before serving. Serve with tortilla chips.

Marni Senner, Long Beach, CA

Easy Slow-Cooker Bean Dip

This dip is perfect to tote to potlucks and family gatherings.

Makes 11 cups

4 16-oz. cans refried beans
1-lb. pkg. Colby Jack cheese, cubed
1-1/4 oz. pkg. taco seasoning mix
1 bunch green onions, chopped
1 c. sour cream
8-oz. pkg. cream cheese, cubed

Place all ingredients in a 3-1/2 quart slow cooker; stir to mix. Cover and cook on low setting 2-1/2 hours. Stir often.

★ HANDY TIP ★ Waiting for your avocados to ripen? Apples speed ripening of peaches, pears, tomatoes, and avocados when stored together in a brown bag. Set in a warm dark place and punch a few holes in the bag for ventilation. They'll ripen more quickly!

Homemade Guacamole

Arlene Smulski, Lyons, IL

Black Forest Fondue

Go retro yet classic with this chocolatey fondue!

Makes 10 servings

3/4 c. whipping cream
1/8 t. salt
1 c. milk chocolate chips
1 c. semi-sweet chocolate chips
2-1/2 T. cherry extract
1 T. corn syrup
pound cake cubes, assorted fruit
　cubes and slices

Bring cream and salt to a boil in a saucepan over medium heat. Remove from heat. Add chocolates to saucepan; cover and let stand 3 to 4 minutes. Uncover; whisk until chocolate mixture is smooth. Whisk in extract and corn syrup. Serve immediately with pound cake and fruit. May be kept warm in a slow cooker or fondue pot over low heat; stir often.

Kenny Phillips, Jacksonville, FL

Antipasto Kabobs

Easy-to-pick-up party food! Add some crunchy bread sticks for a light warm-weather meal.

Makes 16 servings

1/3 c. olive oil
1/3 c. balsamic vinegar
1 T. fresh thyme, minced
1 clove garlic, minced
1 t. sugar
9-oz. pkg. cheese-filled tortellini,
　cooked
5-oz. pkg. thinly sliced salami
12-oz. jar artichoke hearts, drained
　and quartered
5-3/4 oz. jar green olives with
　pimentos, drained
16-oz. jar banana peppers, drained
1 pt. cherry tomatoes
16 6-inch skewers, soaked in water

Combine oil, vinegar, thyme, garlic and sugar; set aside. Thread remaining ingredients onto skewers alternately in order given. Arrange skewers in a single layer in a glass or plastic container; drizzle with marinade. Cover and refrigerate for 2 to 3 hours, turning occasionally. Drain and discard marinade before serving.

Black Forest Fondue

Tammy Rowe, Fremont, OH

Scrumptious Stuffed Potato Skins

Scrumptious says it all! Plus...this easy-to-make appetizer will satisfy a hungry crowd.

Makes 16

4 baking potatoes, quartered
 lengthwise
olive oil
8-oz. container sour cream
1/3 c. shredded Cheddar cheese
1 t. garlic, minced
1 green onion, chopped
2 t. dried parsley
2 T. bacon bits
1/2 t. salt
1/2 t. pepper
Garnish: bacon bits, chopped
 green onions, shredded
 Cheddar cheese

Brush potato skins with olive oil; arrange on an ungreased baking sheet cut-side up. Bake at 400 degrees for 30 minutes; cool. Scoop out insides of potatoes, leaving about 1/8-inch shells; reserve scooped-out potato for another use. Combine remaining ingredients except garnish and spoon into potato skins; return to baking sheet. Bake an additional 20 minutes. Garnish with additional bacon bits, green onions and Cheddar cheese.

Judy Borecky, Escondido, CA

Mushroom Turnovers

A super make-ahead recipe! Freeze unbaked turnovers on baking sheets, then store in freezer bags. At serving time, bake as directed.

Makes 5 dozen

8-oz. pkg. cream cheese, softened
1 c. plus 2 T. margarine, divided
2 c. plus 2 T. all-purpose flour, divided
4 c. sliced mushrooms, chopped
2/3 c. green onions, chopped
1/3 c. sour cream
1/4 t. dried thyme
1/4 t. salt
1 egg white, beaten
Garnish: sesame seed

Blend cream cheese, one cup margarine and 2 cups flour; chill. In a skillet, sauté mushrooms and onions in remaining margarine for 3 minutes. Add sour cream, remaining flour, thyme and salt. Cook for several more minutes, stirring occasionally. Divide chilled dough in half; roll out 1/8-inch thick and cut with a 2-1/2" round cutter. Place a heaping 1/4 teaspoon mushroom mixture in center of each circle. Fold over; press edges gently with fingers to seal. Use a spatula to transfer turnovers to a lightly greased baking sheet; press edges with a fork. Brush turnovers with egg white; sprinkle with sesame seed. Bake at 350 degrees for 20 minutes.

Scrumptious Stuffed Potato Skins

Francine Kepler, Bellefontaine, OH

Fresh Salsa

This garden-fresh favorite can be made ahead. The flavors only improve over time.

Makes 3-1/2 cups

1 jalapeño pepper, seeded and minced
1 cucumber, peeled and diced
4 plum tomatoes, chopped
1/2 c. fresh cilantro, finely chopped
2 T. vinegar
2 T. olive oil
1 t. sugar
1 t. ground cumin
1/2 t. salt
tortilla chips

Stir together all ingredients except tortilla chips in a small bowl. Cover and chill at least one hour. Serve with tortilla chips.

Cindy McKinnon, El Dorado, AR

Cheese Straws

My Aunt Sister's famous signature recipe. She passed away several years ago, yet she is still remembered as being an awesome cook.

Makes 3 to 4 dozen

16-oz. pkg. shredded sharp Cheddar
  cheese, at room temperature
1-1/4 c. margarine, softened
3 c. all-purpose flour
1 t. cayenne pepper
1 t. salt

Combine all ingredients together in a large bowl. Mix well, using your hands. Spoon dough into a cookie press with a star tip. Press dough in strips onto ungreased baking sheets; cut strips 3 inches long. Bake at 350 degrees for 12 to 15 minutes, or until orange on bottom and around edges. Cool on wire racks; store in an airtight container.

Fresh Salsa

Morgan Ferguson, Altoona, PA

Baked Spinach & Artichoke Dip

This creamy dip is sure to be a hit at any tailgating party. You may even want to double the recipe!

Makes 11 servings

2 6-oz. pkgs. baby spinach
1 T. butter
8-oz. pkg. Neufchâtel cheese
1 clove garlic, chopped
14-oz. can artichoke hearts, drained and chopped
1/2 c. light sour cream
1/2 c. shredded mozzarella cheese, divided
pita wedges or pita chips

Microwave spinach in a large microwave-safe bowl on high 3 minutes or until wilted; drain well. Press spinach between paper towels to remove excess moisture. Chop spinach. Melt butter in a non-stick skillet over medium-high heat. Add Neufchâtel cheese and garlic; cook 3 to 4 minutes, stirring constantly, until cheese melts. Fold in spinach, artichokes, sour cream and 1/4 cup mozzarella cheese; stir until mozzarella cheese melts. Transfer mixture to a shallow one-quart casserole dish. Sprinkle with remaining mozzarella cheese. Bake at 350 degrees for 15 minutes or until hot and bubbly. Serve immediately with pita wedges or pita chips.

Anna McMaster, Portland, OR

Tomato-Bacon Nibbles

A 1/4-teaspoon measuring spoon is just right for scooping out tiny tomatoes for stuffng.

Makes 2 to 2-1/2 dozen

24 to 30 cherry tomatoes
16-oz. pkg. bacon, crisply cooked and crumbled
2 T. fresh parsley, chopped
1/2 c. green onions, finely chopped
3 T. grated Parmesan cheese
1/2 c. mayonnaise

Cut a thin slice off the top of each tomato and, if desired, cut a thin slice from bottom of each tomato (so tomatoes will stand upright); scoop out and discard tomato pulp. Place tomatoes upside-down on a paper towel to drain 10 minutes. Mix bacon and remaining ingredients in a small bowl; stuff tomatoes. Serve immediately or chill up to 2 hours.

★ BITE SIZE ★ For stand-up parties, make it easy on guests by serving foods that can be eaten in just one or two bites. Tomato-Bacon Nibbles are perfect. Also try mini bruschetta toasts and guacamole spooned into scoop-type tortilla chips too!

Baked Spinach & Artichoke Dip

Sue Bronson, Thornville, OH

Patchwork Wheel of Brie

A festive centerpiece for your appetizer table.

Serves 20 to 25

5-lb. round of Brie cheese
1/2 c. sweetened dried cranberries
　or dried currants
1/2 c. walnuts, finely chopped
1/2 c. fresh dill or chives, chopped
1/4 c. poppy seed
1 c. sliced almonds
toasted bread rounds

Remove the rind from the top of the cheese by cutting carefully with a sharp knife. Lightly score the top of the cheese into 10 equal pie-shaped sections. Sprinkle half of each of the toppings onto each wedge and press gently until you have decorated all 10 sections. Allow to stand at room temperature for at least 40 minutes before serving. Serve with bread rounds.

Rhonda Johnson, Studio City, CA

Bruschetta with Cranberry Relish

Serve these crisp, savory slices at your next Thanksgiving feast...you may just start a new tradition!

Makes 18 to 20 servings

1 French baguette loaf, sliced
　1/4-inch thick
1 to 2 T. olive oil
1 t. orange zest
1 t. lemon zest
1/2 c. chopped pecans
1/2 c. crumbled blue cheese

Brush baguette slices lightly with oil. Arrange on a broiler pan; toast lightly under broiler. Turn slices over; spread with Cranberry Relish. Sprinkle with zests, pecans and blue cheese. Place under broiler just until cheese begins to melt.

Cranberry Relish:

16-oz. can whole-berry cranberry
　sauce
6-oz. pkg. sweetened dried
　cranberries
1/2 c. sugar
1 t. rum extract
1 c. chopped pecans

Stir all ingredients together.

Patchwork Wheel of Brie

Angela Murphy, Tempe, AZ

Fried Cheese Sticks

Just about everyone loves fried cheese sticks. My version gets a punch of heat from cayenne pepper and cheese spiced with jalapeños. To tame the heat, use plain Monterey Jack (without the peppers), mozzarella or Swiss cheese, and either omit the cayenne pepper or use less of it.

Makes 28 appetizers

2 8-oz. pkgs. Monterey Jack
   cheese with jalapeño peppers
1 c. all-purpose flour
1-1/2 t. cayenne pepper
1 c. fine dry bread crumbs
1 t. dried parsley
4 eggs, beaten
oil for frying
Optional: marinara sauce

Cut cheese crosswise into 3/4-inch slices. Lay slices flat and cut in half lengthwise. Combine flour and cayenne pepper; stir well. Combine bread crumbs and parsley in another bowl; stir well. Dip cheese sticks in beaten eggs. Dredge in flour mixture. Dip coated cheese in egg again; dredge in bread crumb mixture, pressing firmly so that crumbs adhere. Place cheese sticks on a wax paper-lined baking sheet and freeze at least 30 minutes. Fry cheese sticks in 375-degree deep oil until golden brown. Drain on paper towels. Serve immediately with marinara sauce, if desired.

★ DOUBLE DIPPING ★ If you're serving up marinara sauce for Fried Cheese Sticks, try dipping warm slices of focaccia or veggie sticks in the marinara sauce too...yummy!

Fried Cheese Sticks

Nancy Johnson, Carmel, IN

Marinated Olives

These olives are quite spicy & will please anyone who loves to nibble on fiery foods!

Makes 2-1/2 cups

6-oz. can pitted ripe olives, drained
6-oz. jar pitted green olives, drained
1 hot chili pepper, minced
3 cloves garlic, minced
1 t. dried oregano
1 c. olive oil

Combine olives, chili pepper, garlic and oregano in a jar with a lid. Cover with olive oil. Shake olives gently and let stand at room temperature overnight. Store in refrigerator and use within one week.

Kathy Grashoff, Fort Wayne, IN

Bacon-Horseradish Dip

Put a slow cooker to work cooking up this creamy, cheesy dip...it's out of this world!

Makes 7 to 8 cups

3 8-oz. pkgs. cream cheese, softened
12-oz. pkg. shredded Cheddar cheese
1 c. half-and-half
1/3 c. green onion, chopped
3 cloves garlic, minced
3 T. prepared horseradish
1 T. Worcestershire sauce
1/2 t. pepper
12 slices bacon, crisply cooked and
    crumbled
bagel chips or assorted crackers

Combine all ingredients except bacon and chips or crackers in a slow cooker. Cover and cook on low setting for 4 to 5 hours, or on high setting for 2 to 2-1/2 hours, stirring once halfway through. Just before serving, stir in bacon. Serve with bagel chips or crackers.

Marinated Olives

Diane Cohen, Breinigsville, PA

Pizza Roll Snacks

Who needs frozen pizza rolls when it's a snap to make these yummy rolls? My girls love them for after-school snacks. If there are any leftovers, they warm up great in the microwave.

Makes 16

8-oz. tube refrigerated crescent
   rolls
3 T. pizza sauce
1/4 c. grated Parmesan cheese
16 slices pepperoni, divided
1/3 c. shredded mozzarella
   cheese, divided
Garnish: small fresh basil leaves

Unroll crescent roll dough but do not separate; press perforations to seal. Spread pizza sauce evenly over dough, leaving a one-inch border. Sprinkle with Parmesan cheese and roll up, starting with the long side. Using a sharp knife, cut roll-up into 16 slices. Place slices cut-side down on a greased baking sheet. Top each slice with one pepperoni slice and one teaspoon mozzarella cheese. Bake at 375 degrees for 9 to 11 minutes, until edges are golden and cheese melts. Garnish with basil leaves.

★ IN A PINCH ★ Whip up some no-cooking-needed pizza sauce in a jiffy. In a blender, combine a can of seasoned diced tomatoes, a little garlic and a shake of Italian seasoning. Purée to the desired consistency.

Pizza Roll Snacks

Emmaline Dunkley, Pine City, MN

Pork & Apple Meatballs

Serve these yummy meatballs immediately or keep warm in a slow cooker until ready to serve.

Serves 8 to 10

1 lb. ground pork sausage
1-1/4 c. pork-flavored stuffing mix
1/2 c. low-sodium chicken broth
1/2 c. Honeycrisp apple, peeled, cored and diced
1/2 c. onion, diced
1 egg, beaten
1-1/2 t. mustard
1/2 c. shredded sharp Cheddar cheese
Optional: barbecue sauce

Combine all ingredients except barbecue sauce in a large bowl. Form into balls by tablespoonfuls. Place on a lightly greased 15"x10" jelly-roll pan. Bake at 350 degrees for 18 to 20 minutes, until meatballs are no longer pink in the middle. Brush with barbecue sauce, if desired.

Jen Stout, Blandon, PA

Savory Bacon Bites

We love to make these skewers every year as soon as sweet onions first arrive on produce stands.

Makes 8 servings

2 sweet onions, each sliced into 8 wedges
8 thick slices hickory-smoked bacon, cut in half
8 6-inch wooden skewers, soaked in water
2 T. brown sugar, packed
2 T. balsamic vinegar
1 T. molasses

Wrap each onion wedge in a bacon slice. Arrange 2 wedges on each skewer; place in a shallow glass or plastic dish. Combine remaining ingredients; drizzle over skewers. Cover and refrigerate for one hour. Remove skewers from marinade, reserving marinade. Grill, covered, over medium-high heat for 20 minutes, or until onions are crisp-tender, occasionally turning and basting with reserved marinade.

Pork & Apple Meatballs

Breakfast Egg Muffins, Page 56

CHAPTER TWO

Breakfast & Brunch

Chocolate Pinwheels, Page 74

Edie's Honeyed Fruit Salad, Page 80

Melynda Hoffman, Fort Wayne, IN

Pecan Pie Muffins

When my daughter Brooke took these muffins to the Allen County Fair, she won a blue ribbon. All the judges asked for another muffin, please! We make them for our holiday breakfasts, but they're a great treat anytime. For a different taste, use coconut oil instead of butter.

Makes 9 muffins

1 c. chopped pecans
1 c. brown sugar, packed
1/2 c. all-purpose flour
2 eggs
1/2 c. butter, melted and cooled
    slightly

Combine pecans, brown sugar and flour in a large bowl and mix well; make a well in the center and set aside. Lightly beat eggs in a separate bowl; stir in butter and mix well. Add to pecan mixture, stirring just until moistened. Grease the bottom of 9 muffin cups; spoon batter into muffin cups, filling 2/3 full. Bake at 350 degrees for 20 to 25 minutes, until golden. Immediately remove from muffin pan; cool on a wire rack.

Emily Johnson, Pocatello, ID

Mom's Applesauce Muffins

These couldn't be easier to make! Add 1/2 cup chopped nuts if you like a little crunch.

Makes 12 to 16 muffins

1/2 c. butter, softened
1 c. sugar
1 c. applesauce
1 egg, beaten
2 c. all-purpose flour
1 t. baking soda
1 t. cinnamon
1/2 t. ground cloves
1/4 t. salt
1 c. raisins

Combine butter, sugar, applesauce and egg. In a separate bowl, combine flour, baking soda, cinnamon, cloves and salt; stir into butter mixture just until moistened. Stir in raisins. Fill paper-lined muffin cups 3/4 full; sprinkle with Crumb Topping. Bake at 350 degrees for 25 to 30 minutes.

Crumb Topping:

1/2 c. butter, softened
3/4 c. all-purpose flour
3/4 c. quick-cooking oats, uncooked
1/2 c. brown sugar, packed
2 t. cinnamon

Blend all ingredients until crumbly.

Pecan Pie Muffins

Staci Meyers, Montezuma, GA

Rosemary-Lemon Scones

Wonderful served warm with butter and jam.

Makes 8 scones

2 c. all-purpose flour
2 T. sugar
1 T. baking powder
2 t. fresh rosemary, chopped
2 t. lemon zest
1/4 t. salt
1/4 c. butter
2 eggs, beaten
1/2 c. plus 1 T. whipping cream, divided
1 t. cinnamon
1 t. coarse sugar

Combine flour, sugar, baking powder, rosemary, lemon zest and salt in a bowl; mix well. Cut in butter until mixture is crumbly; set aside. Combine eggs with 1/2 cup whipping cream in a separate bowl and mix well; add to flour mixture and stir. Dough should be sticky. Turn dough out onto a well-floured surface; gently knead 10 times and shape into an 8-inch circle about one-inch thick. Cut circle into wedges and place on a lightly greased baking sheet. Brush with remaining whipping cream. Sprinkle with cinnamon and coarse sugar. Bake at 400 degrees for 15 minutes, or until golden.

Regina Ferrigno, Delaware, OH

Grammy's Oatmeal-Buttermilk Pancakes

Whenever we visit Grammy, these yummy pancakes are on the breakfast table without fail...usually surrounded by sausage or bacon, scrambled eggs and toast with jam. We can't imagine breakfast any other way!

Makes 2 dozen

2 c. long-cooking oats, uncooked
2 c. plus 1/4 c. buttermilk, divided
1/2 c. all-purpose flour
1/2 c. whole-wheat flour
2 t. sugar
1-1/2 t. baking powder
1-1/2 t. baking soda
1 t. salt
2 eggs
2 T. butter, melted and cooled
Garnish: butter, warm maple syrup

Combine oats and 2 cups buttermilk in a bowl; cover and refrigerate overnight. To prepare pancakes, sift together flours, sugar, baking powder, baking soda and salt. Set aside. Beat together eggs and butter in a large bowl. Stir egg mixture into oat mixture. Add flour mixture, stirring well. If batter is too thick, stir in 2 to 4 tablespoons remaining buttermilk. Pour batter by heaping tablespoonfuls onto a well-greased hot griddle. Cook until bubbles appear on the surface; flip and continue cooking until golden. Top with butter and maple syrup.

Rosemary-Lemon Scones

Linda Davidson, Lexington, KY

Cinnamon-Apple Muffins

These muffins are scrumptious served warm with butter...they make any meal a little more special!

Makes one dozen

2 c. all-purpose flour
1 T. baking powder
1 t. cinnamon
1/2 t. allspice
1/8 t. salt
3 T. brown sugar, packed
3 T. butter, melted
3/4 c. milk
2 T. mayonnaise
2 apples, peeled, cored and grated
1/3 c. raisins
1/3 c. chopped walnuts

Sift flour, baking powder, cinnamon, allspice and salt into a large bowl. Add remaining ingredients and mix well; batter will be thick. Spoon batter into 12 paper-lined muffin cups. Bake at 400 degrees for 20 minutes, or until centers spring back when touched. Remove from pan and cool on a wire rack; serve warm.

Gretchen Hickman, Galva, IL

Country Biscuits Supreme

These are good with butter and honey...terrific with beef stew.

Makes 12 to 15

2 c. all-purpose flour
4 t. baking powder
2 t. sugar
1/2 t. salt
1/2 t. cream of tartar
1/2 c. shortening
2/3 c. milk

Sift flour, baking powder, sugar, salt and cream of tartar into a large bowl. Cut in shortening until mixture is crumbly. Add milk and stir just until moistened. Turn dough out onto a lightly floured surface; knead gently 30 seconds and roll out to 1/2-inch thickness. Cut with floured biscuit cutter and place on an ungreased baking sheet. Bake at 425 degrees for 10 to 12 minutes, until golden.

★ HANDY TIP ★ For best results, be sure to use the type of fat named in the recipe. Butter bakes up well and gives muffins wonderful flavor. Avoid light or whipped margarine when baking. If shortening is called for, look for it in easy-to-measure sticks.

Cinnamon-Apple Muffins

Jill Ball, Highland, UT

Jill's Banana Butter

Pumpkin pie spice makes this a great fall breakfast butter...spread it on toast, English muffins or bagels.

Makes 3 cups

4 ripe bananas, sliced
3 T. lemon juice
1-1/2 c. sugar
1 t. pumpkin pie spice

Place bananas and lemon juice in a food processor; pulse until smooth. Transfer mixture to a saucepan and stir in remaining ingredients. Bring to a boil over medium-high heat. Reduce heat and simmer 15 minutes; stir often. Spoon into an airtight container; cover and keep refrigerated.

Peg Baker, La Rue, OH

Orange Biscuits

My grandmother kept a journal and always included lots of recipes alongside her memories. I remember her always serving these with ham... oh, the aroma from the kitchen was wonderful!

Makes one dozen

1/2 c. orange juice
3/4 c. sugar, divided
1/2 c. butter, divided
2 t. orange zest
2 c. all-purpose flour
1 t. baking powder
1/2 t. salt
1/3 c. shortening
3/4 c. milk
1/2 t. cinnamon

Combine orange juice, 1/2 cup sugar, 1/4 cup butter and orange zest in a medium saucepan. Cook and stir over medium heat for 2 minutes. Fill 12 ungreased muffin cups each with 1-1/4 tablespoons of mixture; set aside. Sift together flour, baking powder and salt; cut in shortening until mixture resembles coarse crumbs. Stir in milk and mix with a fork until mixture forms a ball. On a heavily floured surface, knead dough for one minute. Roll into a 9-inch square about 1/2-inch thick; spread with softened butter. Combine cinnamon and remaining sugar; sprinkle over dough. Roll up dough and cut into 12 slices about 3/4-inch thick. Place slices, cut-side down, in muffin cups. Bake at 450 degrees for 14 to 17 minutes. Cool for 2 to 3 minutes; remove from pan.

Jill's Banana Butter

Joyceann Dreibelbis, Wooster, OH

Breakfast Egg Muffins

Make a large batch of these muffins and have a healthy to-go breakfast anytime. These tasty morsels can be wrapped and frozen, then just popped into the microwave for a quick hot breakfast.

Makes one dozen

1/2 c. mushrooms, diced
1 T. butter
7 eggs
2 c. shredded Cheddar cheese
1 c. cooked ham, bacon or sausage, diced
1/2 c. baby spinach, finely shredded
2 to 3 T. onion, chopped
2 T. green pepper, diced
2 T. red pepper, diced
salt and pepper to taste
Optional: grated Parmesan cheese

In a skillet over medium heat, sauté mushrooms in butter until tender; remove from heat and cool slightly. In a large bowl, beat eggs until smooth. Add mushrooms and remaining ingredients; mix well. Ladle egg mixture evenly into 12 greased muffin cups. Top with Parmesan cheese, if desired. Bake at 350 degrees for 25 minutes, or until set. Cool slightly before removing muffins from pan.

Christine Schnaufer, Geneseo, IL

Cheddar Biscuits

This quick-to-fix breakfast is perfect for those chilly mornings when you need something to fill you up and keep you warm.

Makes 6 servings

2-1/4 c. biscuit baking mix
1/2 c. shredded Cheddar cheese
2 T. fresh parsley, chopped
1/3 c. milk
1/4 c. sour cream
2 T. Dijon mustard
1 egg, beaten

Combine baking mix, cheese and parsley in a large bowl; stir just until blended. Combine milk, sour cream and mustard in a small bowl; stir well. Add sour cream mixture to baking mix mixture, stirring just until blended. Place dough on a lightly floured surface; knead 10 times. Pat dough into a 1/2-inch-thick circle; cut with a 2-inch biscuit cutter. Arrange biscuits on ungreased baking sheets; brush tops lightly with beaten egg. Bake at 425 degrees for 12 to 15 minutes, until golden. Serve warm.

Breakfast Egg Muffins

Elizabeth McCord, Memphis, TN

Fruit & Nut Granola Bars

Granola bars are a favorite snack for kids and adults alike. These delicious bars are packed full of good stuff...so easy to make at home that you'll never buy them at the store again!

Makes 16 bars

1-3/4 c. quick-cooking oats, uncooked
3/4 c. crispy rice cereal
1/2 c. brown sugar, packed
1/3 c. all-purpose flour
1/2 t. salt
1/2 t. cinnamon
1/2 c. shredded coconut
1 c. chopped walnuts
3/4 c. slivered almonds
3/4 c. raisins
5-oz. pkg. sweetened dried cherries
5-oz. pkg. sweetened dried cranberries
1/2 c. mini semi-sweet chocolate chips
2/3 c. canola oil
1/3 c. creamy peanut butter
1/3 c. honey
1/4 c. hot water
2 t. vanilla extract

In a large bowl, combine oats, cereal, brown sugar, flour, salt, cinnamon and coconut; toss well. Add nuts, dried fruits and chocolate chips. Toss again; set aside. In a small bowl, mix together remaining ingredients; spoon over oat mixture and mix well. Divide between 2 greased 11"x7" baking pans; press down to flatten. Bake, uncovered, at 350 degrees for 20 to 22 minutes, until edges are golden. Let cool in pans. Cut into bars and store in an airtight container.

★ MAKE AHEAD ★ Half-pint Mason jars are just right for filling with layers of fresh fruit, creamy yogurt and crumbled granola bars. They can even be popped into the fridge the night before, then topped with granola just before serving. Add a spoon and breakfast is served!

Fruit & Nut Granola Bars

Sherrie Loncon, Orange, TX

Chicken-Fried Bacon

I came across this recipe while traveling many, many years ago in San Antonio, Texas. The taste is indescribably good!

Serves 8 to 10

**2 eggs, beaten
1 c. milk
1 c. all-purpose flour
salt and pepper to taste
1 lb. bacon
1/2 c. shortening
Garnish: ranch salad dressing**

Whisk together eggs and milk in a shallow bowl; set aside. Blend flour, salt and pepper in a separate bowl. Dip each slice of bacon into egg mixture; roll in seasoned flour. Melt shortening in a skillet over medium heat. Add bacon, a few slices at a time. Cook until crisp and golden; drain. Serve with ranch dressing.

Vickie, Gooseberry Patch

Sausage Gravy & Biscuits

Enjoy these light & fluffy biscuits topped with hot sausage gravy any time of the day.

Serves 10 to 12

**1/2 c. all-purpose flour
2 lbs. ground pork sausage, browned
  and drained
4 c. milk
salt and pepper to taste
Biscuits**

In a large skillet, sprinkle flour over sausage, stirring until flour is dissolved. Gradually stir in milk and cook over medium heat until thick and bubbly. Season with salt and pepper; serve over warm Biscuits.

Biscuits:

**4 c. self-rising flour
2 T. sugar
3 T. baking powder
7 T. shortening
2 c. buttermilk**

Sift together flour, sugar and baking powder; cut in shortening. Mix in buttermilk with a fork, just until dough is moistened. Shape dough into a ball and knead a few times on a lightly floured surface. Roll out to 3/4-inch thickness and cut with a 3-inch biscuit cutter. Place biscuits on a greased baking sheet. Bake at 450 degrees for about 15 minutes or until golden. Makes 2 dozen.

Chicken-Fried Bacon

Andrea Hickerson, Trenton, TN

Bacon Breakfast Casserole

This is one of my most versatile recipes! It can be made up to a day ahead of time with just about any type of bread, breakfast meat and cheese you like. Simply refrigerate it until you're ready to bake.

Serves 8 to 10

6 slices white bread
1 lb. bacon, crisply cooked and
    crumbled
8 eggs, beaten
3 c. milk
1/4 t. salt
1/4 t. pepper
1/4 t. garlic powder
8-oz. pkg. shredded Cheddar cheese

Spray a 13"x9" baking pan with non-stick vegetable spray. Lay bread slices in the bottom of pan; spread bacon evenly over bread and set aside. In a large bowl, whisk together eggs, milk and seasonings; pour over bread. Spread cheese evenly over top. Bake, uncovered, at 350 degrees for 30 minutes, or until set. Cut into squares.

Lori Ritchey, Denver, PA

Garden-Fresh Zucchini Quiche

A delicious way to use up your garden's bounty of zucchini!

Makes 8 servings

4 c. zucchini, grated
1-1/2 c. biscuit baking mix
1/2 c. oil
3 eggs, beaten
1 t. dried oregano
1/2 t. salt
1/2 t. pepper
1-1/2 c. shredded Cheddar cheese
1/2 c. onion, chopped

In a large bowl, mix together zucchini, baking mix, oil and eggs until well blended. Add remaining ingredients. Pour into a lightly greased 9" deep-dish pie plate. Bake at 400 degrees for 25 minutes.

★ GARDEN-FRESH ★ Have an overabundance of tomatoes, zucchini or peppers in your garden? Set veggies out in bushel baskets at an end-of-summer party along with paper sacks...invite guests to fill the sacks and take 'em home as party favors!

Bacon Breakfast Casserole

Jo Ann, Gooseberry Patch

Chocolate Chip Coffee Cake

I love this easy coffee cake recipe... you will too! It goes together in minutes and makes enough for a family gathering, a church reception or everyone in the office.

Makes 16 servings

18-1/2 oz. pkg. yellow cake mix
8-oz. container sour cream
3 eggs, beaten
3/4 c. water

Combine all ingredients in a large bowl. Beat with an electric mixer on low speed until moistened. Turn to high speed; beat for 2 minutes, or until well mixed. Spread 2/3 of batter in a greased and lightly floured 13"x9" baking pan. Sprinkle with half of Streusel Topping. Repeat layering with remaining batter and topping. Bake at 350 degrees for 35 to 45 minutes, until a toothpick inserted in the center tests done.

Streusel Topping:

1 c. brown sugar, packed
2 T. all-purpose flour
2 T. butter, melted
2 t. cinnamon
1/2 c. semi-sweet chocolate chips
1/2 c. chopped walnuts

Combine all ingredients in a bowl; mix well.

★ BRUNCH BUNCH ★ Planning a midday brunch? Along with breakfast foods like baked eggs, coffee cake and cereal, offer a light, savory main dish or two for those who have already enjoyed breakfast.

Chocolate Chip Coffee Cake

Wendy Ball, Battle Creek, MI

Good-for-You Morning Melts

I used to make these breakfast sandwiches for my husband and myself when we were newly married. It always made our small kitchen warm and cozy with just the two of us. Now I sometimes use bagel thins or sandwich thins instead of English muffins. They turn out a bit crisper, yet still make you feel warm inside.

Makes 8 servings

**4 English muffins, split
 and toasted
1 T. Dijon mustard
8 slices Canadian bacon
1-1/2 Honeycrisp or Fuji apples,
 cored and thinly sliced
8 slices favorite cheese**

Spread cut sides of muffin halves with mustard; place on an ungreased baking sheet. Top each with bacon, apple and cheese slices. Bake at 350 degrees for 6 to 8 minutes, until cheese melts. Serve hot.

J.J. Presley, Portland, TX

Cheesy Sausage-Potato Casserole

Top with salsa and a dollop of sour cream just for fun!

Serves 6 to 8

**3 to 4 potatoes, sliced
14-oz. smoked pork sausage, sliced
 into 2-inch lengths
1 onion, chopped
1/2 c. butter, sliced
1 c. shredded Cheddar cheese
Garnish: chopped green onions**

Layer potatoes, sausage and onion in a 13"x9" baking pan sprayed with non-stick vegetable spray. Dot with butter; sprinkle with cheese. Bake, uncovered, at 350 degrees for 1-1/2 hours. Garnish with green onions.

★ FAVORITE FLAVORS ★ **Quick-cooking** smoked sausages are a great choice for breakfast or brunch. Different flavors like hickory-smoked or cheese-filled sausage can really jazz up a recipe too.

Good-for-You Morning Melts

Linda Jackson, Battle Creek, MI

Tangy Cranberry Breakfast Cake

This yummy coffee cake has three fantastic layers!

Makes 12 servings

2 c. all-purpose flour
1-1/3 c. sugar, divided
1-1/2 t. baking powder
1/2 t. baking soda
1/4 t. salt
2 eggs, divided
3/4 c. orange juice
1/4 c. butter, melted
2 t. vanilla extract, divided
2 c. cranberries, coarsely chopped
Optional: 1 T. orange zest
8-oz. pkg. cream cheese, softened

Combine flour, one cup sugar, baking powder, baking soda and salt in a large bowl; mix well and set aside. Combine one egg, orange juice, butter and one teaspoon vanilla in a small bowl; mix well and stir into flour mixture until well combined. Fold in cranberries and zest, if using. Pour into a greased 9" round springform pan and set aside. Beat together cream cheese and remaining sugar in a small bowl until smooth. Add remaining egg and vanilla; mix well. Spread over batter; sprinkle with Topping. Place pan on a baking sheet; bake at 350 degrees for one hour, or until toothpick inserted in center comes out clean. Let cool on wire rack for 15 minutes before removing sides of pan.

Topping:

6 T. all-purpose flour
1/4 c. sugar
2 T. butter, diced

Combine flour and sugar in a small bowl. Cut in butter with a pastry blender or fork until crumbly.

★ FREEZER FRIENDLY ★ Fresh cranberries can be kept frozen up to 12 months, so if you enjoy them, stock up every autumn when they're available and pop unopened bags in the freezer. You'll be able to add their fruity tang to recipes all year 'round.

Tangy Cranberry Breakfast Cake

Hattie Douthit, Crawford, NE

No-Knead Oatmeal Bread

Spread peanut butter or softened butter on this slightly sweet and so-yummy favorite.

Makes 2 loaves

2 envs. active dry yeast
1/2 c. warm water
1 c. quick-cooking oats, uncooked
1/2 c. light molasses
1/3 c. shortening
1-1/2 c. boiling water
1 T. salt
6-1/4 c. all-purpose flour, divided
2 eggs, beaten

Dissolve yeast in warm water (110 to 115 degrees) in a small bowl; let stand about 5 minutes. Combine oats, molasses, shortening, boiling water and salt in a large bowl; stir until shortening is melted. Cool until lukewarm. Stir in 2 cups flour; add eggs and beat well. Stir in yeast mixture. Add remaining flour, 2 cups at a time, mixing well after each addition until a stiff dough forms. Beat vigorously about 10 minutes, until smooth. Place dough in a lightly greased bowl, turning to coat top. Cover tightly; place in refrigerator at least 2 hours to overnight. Turn dough out onto a floured surface. Form into 2 loaves; place seam-side down in greased 8"x4" loaf pans. Cover; let rise in a warm place (85 degrees), free from drafts, 2 hours, until double in bulk. Bake at 375 degrees for about 40 minutes. If top begins to brown too fast, cover with aluminum foil during last half of baking time.

★ FRESH IS BEST ★ If the baking powder, baking soda and yeast have been in the cupboard since last year, it's best to replace them...spices too.

No-Knead Oatmeal Bread

Kathy Grashoff, Fort Wayne, IN

Kathy's Bacon Popovers

Mmm...bacon! An easy tote-along breakfast to enjoy on the go.

Makes one dozen

2 eggs
1 c. milk
1 T. oil
1 c. all-purpose flour
1/2 t. salt
3 slices bacon, crisply cooked
   and crumbled

Whisk together eggs, milk and oil. Beat in flour and salt just until smooth. Fill 12 greased and floured muffin cups 2/3 full. Sprinkle bacon evenly over batter. Bake at 400 degrees for 25 to 30 minutes, until puffed and golden. Serve warm.

Laura Phares, Greenfield, IN

Hearty Sausage & Egg Bake

This easy-to-fix dish is always a big hit when I serve it at our church's sunrise breakfast...everyone just loves it!

Makes 16 servings

6-oz. pkg. croutons
2 lbs. ground pork breakfast sausage,
   browned and drained
6 eggs
2-1/2 c. milk
1 t. dry mustard
10-3/4 oz. can cream of mushroom
   soup
8-oz. pkg. shredded Cheddar cheese

The night before, sprinkle croutons into a greased 13"x9" baking pan; top with sausage. Beat eggs, milk and mustard in a bowl; pour over sausage. Cover and refrigerate overnight. In the morning, spread soup over casserole; sprinkle with cheese. Bake, uncovered, at 300 degrees for one hour, or until center is done.

Kathy's Bacon Popovers

Lisa Ashton, Aston, PA

Chocolate Pinwheels

We love to serve this with warm spiced milk.

Makes 16 pinwheels

11-oz. tube refrigerated bread sticks
3/4 c. semi-sweet chocolate chips
1/4 c. butter, melted
1/2 c. sugar

Unroll bread sticks and cut them in half. Press chocolate chips in a single row along top of each bread stick half; roll up into a pinwheel. Arrange pinwheels on a parchment paper-lined baking sheet. Brush with melted butter; sprinkle with sugar. Bake at 350 degrees for 10 to 12 minutes, until golden.

Geneva Rogers, Gillette, WY

Orange-Glazed Chocolate Rolls

You'll love the flavors of orange and chocolate in these sweet rolls!

Makes about 1-1/2 dozen

3 c. all-purpose flour, divided
2 envs. active dry yeast
1 t. salt
1 t. cinnamon
1-1/4 c. water
1/3 c. sugar
1/3 c. butter
1 egg
Optional: 1/2 c. raisins
1 c. semi-sweet chocolate chips

Stir together 1-1/2 cups flour, yeast, salt and cinnamon in a large bowl. Combine water, sugar and butter in a saucepan over medium-low heat, stirring constantly until butter is almost melted (115 to 120 degrees). Add sugar mixture to flour mixture; blend until smooth. Mix in egg; stir in remaining flour. Fold in raisins, if desired; cover dough and let rise in a warm place (85 degrees), free from drafts, for one hour, until double in bulk. Punch down dough; let rest for 10 minutes. Fold in chocolate chips; fill greased muffin cups 2/3 full. Cover; let rise until double in bulk. Bake at 425 degrees for 10 to 15 minutes, until golden. Remove from pan and cool completely. Drizzle with Glaze before serving.

Glaze:

1/2 c. powdered sugar
3 t. orange juice

Combine sugar and juice in a small bowl; stir until smooth and creamy.

Chocolate Pinwheels

Gail Blain, Grand Island, NE

Toasted Pecan Pancakes

These very special little pancakes make an ordinary weekend breakfast extraordinary. My kids really enjoy them served with pure maple syrup and sliced ripe bananas on the side!

Makes about 1-1/2 dozen

2 eggs
2 T. sugar
1/4 c. butter, melted and slightly
  cooled
1/4 c. maple syrup
1-1/2 c. all-purpose flour
2 t. baking powder
1/2 t. salt
1-1/2 c. milk
2/3 c. chopped pecans, toasted
2 to 3 t. oil
Garnish: additional butter,
  warmed maple syrup

Beat together eggs, sugar, butter and syrup in a large bowl. Mix together flour, baking powder and salt in a separate bowl. Add flour mixture and milk alternately to egg mixture, beginning and ending with flour mixture. Stir in pecans. Set a griddle or a large, heavy skillet over medium heat and brush lightly with oil. Griddle is ready when a few drops of water sizzle when sprinkled on the surface. Pour batter by scant 1/4 cupfuls onto griddle. Cook until bubbles appear on top of pancakes and bottoms are golden, about 2 minutes. Flip and cook on the other side, about one more minute, until golden. Add a little more oil to griddle for each batch. Serve pancakes with additional butter and warm maple syrup.

★ SPICE IT UP ★ Keep a tin of apple pie spice on hand to jazz up pancakes, muffins and coffee cakes...a quick shake adds cinnamon, nutmeg and allspice all at once.

Toasted Pecan Pancakes

Debra Alf, Robbinsdale, MN

Jumbo Quiche Muffins

These handheld breakfast treats are perfect to tote along when rushing out the door before school. The kids will love them!

Makes 8 muffins

16.3-oz. tube refrigerated flaky buttermilk biscuits
1/2 c. cream cheese, softened
4 eggs, beaten
1/4 t. seasoned salt
1/4 t. pepper
6 slices bacon, crisply cooked and crumbled
1/2 c. shredded Cheddar cheese

Place each biscuit into a greased jumbo muffin cup; press to form a well. Combine cream cheese, eggs, salt and pepper. Spoon 3 tablespoons egg mixture into each biscuit well; sprinkle with bacon and top with cheese. Bake at 375 degrees for 15 minutes.

Angie Venable, Ostrander, OH

Cheese-Stuffed Biscuits

My kind of recipe...down-home goodness, ready to serve in a jiffy!

Makes 10 biscuits

10-oz. tube refrigerated flaky biscuits
8-oz. pkg. Cheddar cheese, sliced into 10 cubes
1 T. milk
1 t. poppy seed

Separate dough into 10 biscuits. Open a small pocket in side of each biscuit; tuck a cheese cube into each pocket. Press dough together to seal well. Place biscuits on an ungreased baking sheet. Cut a deep "X" in top of each biscuit. Brush with milk and sprinkle with poppy seed. Bake at 400 degrees for 10 to 12 minutes, until golden. Serve warm.

★ FLAVOR TWIST ★ Maple-flavored bacon or peppered bacon gives a nice change of taste to recipes!

Jumbo Quiche Muffins

Edie DeSpain, Logan, UT

Edie's Honeyed Fruit Salad

This salad looks so pretty in my large ceramic watermelon bowl. You could also serve it in a carved watermelon half. A refreshing use for ripe fruit!

Serves 12 to 14

2 cantaloupes or honeydew melons, peeled and cubed
1 watermelon, peeled and cubed
2 qts. strawberries, hulled and sliced
2 qts. blueberries
1 qt. raspberries
2 lbs. peaches, peeled, pitted and sliced
2 lbs. nectarines, peeled, pitted and sliced
2 lbs. seedless red grapes
1 c. maraschino cherries, drained and halved
honey or sugar to taste

In a very large serving bowl, combine all fruit. Add a little honey or sugar to taste. Toss to mix.

Michelle Case, Yardley, PA

Breakfast Berry Parfait

So pretty served in parfait glasses or champagne flutes!

Makes 2 servings

1 c. strawberries, hulled and sliced
1/2 c. raspberries
1/4 c. blackberries
1 c. bran & raisin cereal
6-oz. container strawberry yogurt

Combine berries in a bowl. Top with cereal. Spoon yogurt over berry mixture.

★ SPREAD THE WORD ★ Mash your favorite fruit and mix with cottage or ricotta cheese for a tasty spread on rolls, toast or biscuits.

Edie's Honeyed Fruit Salad

Melody Taynor, Everett, WA

Sunrise Skillet

When our kids want to camp out in the backyard, I just have to wake them to the aroma of a delicious breakfast...and this recipe does the trick every time.

Serves 6 to 8

1/2 lb. bacon
4 c. potatoes, peeled and cubed
1/2 onion, chopped
6 eggs, beaten
1 c. shredded Cheddar cheese
Optional: chopped green onions

Cook bacon in a cast-iron skillet over the slow-burning coals of a campfire or on a stove over medium heat until crisply cooked. Remove bacon from skillet; set aside. Stir potatoes and onion into drippings. Cover and cook until potatoes are tender, about 10 to 12 minutes. Crumble bacon into potatoes. Stir in eggs; cover and cook until set, about 2 minutes. Sprinkle with cheese and onions, if desired; let stand until cheese melts.

Jill Valentine, Jackson, TN

Sausage Brunch Bake

A favorite dish in our family!

Serves 8 to 10

3 c. herb-flavored croutons
8-oz. pkg. shredded Cheddar cheese, divided
1/2 lb. ground pork breakfast sausage, browned and drained
4 eggs, beaten
2-1/2 c. milk, divided
3/4 t. dry mustard
10-3/4 oz. can cream of mushroom soup
32-oz. pkg. frozen shredded hashbrowns, thawed

Spread croutons in an aluminum foil-lined 13"x9" baking pan. Top croutons with 1-1/2 cups cheese and sausage; set aside. Combine eggs, 2 cups milk and mustard; pour over all. Cover and refrigerate overnight. Combine soup with remaining milk; pour over mixture. Spread hashbrowns over top; sprinkle with remaining cheese. Bake, uncovered, at 325 degrees for one hour.

★ BRUNCH BUNCH ★ Serving a bunch for brunch? It's so easy to make individual-size omelets. Just pour ingredients into lightly greased muffin cups and bake for 20 to 25 minutes at 375 degrees, or until centers are set.

Sunrise Skillet

Sue Cherry, Starkville, MS

Rise & Shine Torte

An easy gourmet meal that will impress your guests...also try it with mushrooms and spinach.

Serves 6 to 8

2 eggs, beaten
1/3 c. milk
2 T. all-purpose flour
1/2 t. salt
1 c. sharp Cheddar cheese, shredded
1 c. Monterey Jack cheese, shredded
4-oz. can diced green chiles

Combine eggs, milk, flour and salt in a large bowl; mix well. Add remaining ingredients, mixing well. Pour into a well-greased 13"x9" baking pan. Bake, uncovered, at 350 degrees for 35 minutes. Cut into small squares to serve.

Carrie O'Shea, Marina del Rey, CA

Country Breakfast Casserole

Add a small can of diced green chiles for extra flavor, if you like!

Makes 8 servings

1 T. oil
4 potatoes, diced
1-1/2 t. salt, divided
1 red pepper, diced
1 green pepper, diced
1 onion, minced
8-oz. pkg. breakfast link sausage, chopped, browned and drained
1-1/2 c. egg substitute
1 c. milk
2 T. all-purpose flour
1/2 t. pepper
1 c. shredded Cheddar cheese

Heat oil in medium skillet. Fry potatoes and one teaspoon salt in oil until golden. Add red and green peppers and onion; cook 5 minutes. Spoon into a greased 13"x9" baking pan and top with sausage. Mix together egg substitute, milk, flour, 1/2 teaspoon salt and pepper in mixing bowl. Pour egg mixture over potato mixture; sprinkle with cheese. Bake, uncovered, at 350 degrees for 30 minutes.

Rise & Shine Torte

Salisbury Meatballs, Page 90

CHAPTER THREE

Mains & Burgers

Black Bean Burgers, Page 102

Shrimp Kabobs, Page 124

Trysha Mapley-Barron, Wasilla, AK

Bratwurst Meatloaf

My family agrees this meatloaf is simply awesome. Wonderful German flavor perfect with mashed potatoes for a truly homey meal. We never have leftovers on this one!

Makes 8 servings

1 lb. lean ground beef
1 lb. bratwurst, removed from
   casings and broken up
1 c. soft bread crumbs
2 cloves garlic, pressed
1-oz. pkg. onion soup mix
8-oz. can tomato sauce
1 egg, beaten
2 T. fresh flat-leaf parsley, chopped
2 T. mustard
1 T. cider vinegar
celery salt and pepper to taste
Garnish: additional mustard
5 slices bacon
1 T. brown sugar, packed

In a large bowl, mix together all ingredients except garnish, bacon and brown sugar. Press into a 9"x5" loaf pan sprayed with non-stick vegetable spray. Spread additional mustard over meatloaf. Arrange bacon slices over top; trim bacon or tuck in the edges on the sides. Press brown sugar onto bacon. Cover and bake at 350 degrees for one hour. Drain off any excess fat; let meatloaf rest 5 minutes before slicing.

Lynda McCormick, Burkburnett, TX

Best Beef Brisket

This brisket is fork-tender and delicious.

Serves 10 to 12

1 t. garlic salt
1 t. garlic powder
1-3/4 t. kosher salt
2 t. pepper
2 T. Worcestershire sauce
5 to 6-lb. beef brisket, trimmed
1/3 c. sugar
1 c. barbecue sauce
1 c. Russian salad dressing

Combine first 5 ingredients; rub into brisket. Tightly wrap brisket in heavy-duty aluminum foil; place in an ungreased 13"x9" baking pan. Bake at 300 degrees for 5 hours. Carefully remove foil from brisket; set brisket aside. Measure one cup of broth; discard any remaining broth. Return brisket to baking pan. Mix together one cup broth, sugar, barbecue sauce and salad dressing; pour over brisket. Bake, covered, at 325 degrees for 30 minutes. Uncover and bake 30 more minutes. Serve with sauce.

Bratwurst Meatloaf

Shirley Howie, Foxboro, MA

Salisbury Meatballs

This comfort food favorite is a quick take on Salisbury steak...it can be made in just over 30 minutes. I like to serve it in bowls, ladled over noodles or rice. A delicious one-dish meal!

Makes 8 servings

2 12-oz. pkgs. frozen Italian-style
   meatballs
3 T. olive oil
1/2 c. onion, sliced
2 T. all-purpose flour
2-1/2 c. chicken or beef broth
3 T. tomato paste
1 t. Dijon mustard
3 T. Worcestershire sauce
salt and pepper to taste
6 c. cooked egg noodles or rice

Place frozen meatballs on a lightly greased rimmed baking sheet. Bake at 350 degrees for 30 minutes. Meanwhile, heat oil in a skillet overmedium heat. Add onion; cook until lightly golden, about 4 minutes. Sprinkle onion with flour; stir to coat and cook another 2 minutes. Stir in remaining ingredients except noodles or rice. Bring to a simmer; cook about 10 minutes. Add baked meatballs to the sauce in skillet; stir to coat. Serve meatballs and sauce over cooked egg noodles or rice.

Theresa Wehmeyer, Rosebud, MO

Aunt Flora's Juicyburgers

Each year after Christmas Eve worship, my husband's whole family would gather at Aunt Flora and Uncle Art's home. There was a bounty of delicious food and their tiny home, including the basement, was filled with family. These sandwiches were always served. I am thankful Aunt Flora shared the recipe with me.

Serves 18 to 20

3 lbs. ground beef
1/2 onion, finely diced
14-oz. bottle catsup
1/4 t. Worcestershire sauce
1 T. lemon juice
2 T. brown sugar, packed
3/4 t. dry mustard
18 to 20 sandwich buns, split

Brown beef and onion in a large skillet over medium heat; drain. Add remaining ingredients except buns. Reduce heat to low; simmer for 10 to 15 minutes to combine flavors. To serve, spoon onto buns.

★ HANDY TIP ★ **Use a potato masher to break up ground beef quickly and evenly as it browns.**

Salisbury Meatballs

Jennifer Stone, Chillicothe, OH

Slow-Cooker Shredded Chicken

This recipe is a great help in my kitchen...it's a big batch of chicken that can stretch into two or more meals. The mixture of chicken breasts and thighs is moist and delicious. I like to add barbecue sauce or taco seasoning to half of the shredded chicken and leave the rest plain to add to pasta dishes.

Makes 16 servings, enough for
2 different recipes

2 lbs. frozen boneless, skinless
  chicken breasts
2 lbs. frozen boneless, skinless
  chicken thighs
salt and pepper to taste
2 c. hot water
4 cubes chicken bouillon
Optional: barbecue sauce, or taco
  seasoning mix and chicken broth

Layer frozen chicken pieces in a 6-quart slow cooker, sprinkling with a little salt and pepper. Pour hot water over all; tuck in bouillon cubes. Cover and cook on low setting for 8 hours, or until chicken is very tender. Remove chicken to a large bowl; cool and shred. Reserve broth in slow cooker for another recipe, if desired, or discard. May add barbecue sauce to shredded chicken, or sauté with taco seasoning and broth, or leave plain for any recipes that call for cooked chicken.

★ SPEEDY SUPPER ★ Keep fast-cooking ramen noodles on hand for quick meals. Make a comforting chicken noodle soup by stirring in shredded chicken and diced veggies.

Slow-Cooker Shredded Chicken

Kelly Cook, Dunedin, FL

Tamale Pie

Ready-made tamales make this pie oh-so quick. This makes enough for a crowd, so it's perfect to take to a church supper or family reunion.

Makes 12 servings

2 15-oz. cans beef tamales, divided
15-oz. can chili, divided
9-1/4 oz. pkg. corn chips, divided
1 onion, minced and divided
2 c. shredded Cheddar cheese, divided

Chop one can of tamales; set aside. Spread one cup chili in the bottom of a greased 2-quart casserole dish; layer half the corn chips, half the onion and chopped tamales on top. Sprinkle with half the cheese; repeat layers, ending with whole tamales topped with cheese. Cover and bake at 350 degrees for one hour. Let stand 10 minutes before serving.

Vickie, Gooseberry Patch

Burgundy Meatloaf

A mixture of ground beef and ground pork can also be used in this slow-cooker recipe.

Serves 6 to 8

2 lbs. ground beef
2 eggs
1 c. soft bread crumbs
1 onion, chopped
1/2 c. Burgundy wine or beef broth
1/2 c. fresh parsley, chopped
1 T. fresh basil, chopped
1-1/2 t. salt
1/4 t. pepper
5 slices bacon
1 bay leaf
8-oz. can tomato sauce

Combine ground beef, eggs, crumbs, onion, wine or broth, herbs and seasonings in a large bowl; mix well and set aside. Criss-cross 3 bacon slices on a 12-inch square of aluminum foil. Form meat mixture into a 6-inch round loaf on top of bacon. Cut remaining bacon slices in half; arrange on top of meatloaf. Place bay leaf on top. Lift meatloaf by aluminum foil into a slow cooker; cover and cook on high setting for one hour. Reduce heat to low setting and continue cooking, covered, for 4 more hours. Remove meatloaf from slow cooker by lifting foil. Place on a serving platter, discarding foil and bay leaf. Warm tomato sauce and spoon over sliced meatloaf.

Tamale Pie

JoAnna Nicoline-Haughey, Berwyn, PA

Baked Ham in Peach Sauce

This ham with its fruity sauce is equally scrumptious served hot at a holiday dinner or cold at a summer picnic.

Makes 10 servings

7-lb. cooked ham
1 t. whole cloves
2 16-oz. cans sliced peaches, drained
10-oz. jar apricot preserves
1 c. dry sherry or apple juice
1 t. orange zest
1/2 t. allspice

Place ham in an ungreased 13"x9" baking pan. Score surface of ham in a diamond pattern; insert cloves. Combine remaining ingredients in a blender or food processor. Process until smooth and pour over ham. Cover ham with aluminum foil. Bake at 325 degrees for 30 minutes, basting occasionally with sauce. Uncover and bake for 30 more minutes; continue to baste. Remove ham to a serving platter; slice and serve with sauce from pan. May be served hot or cold.

Lauren Williams, Kewanee, MO

Cola Ham for a Crowd

Always a favorite at any of our family gatherings...especially Christmas. The ham falls off the bone, has wonderful texture and is so delicious.

Serves 12 to 16

8-lb. bone-in ham
12-oz. can cola

Place ham cut-side down in a large slow cooker, trimming to fit if needed. Pour cola over ham. Cover and cook on low setting for 8 to 10 hours.

★ SAVVY SIDE ★ Baked sweet potatoes are yummy with baked ham. Pierce potatoes several times with a fork, and put them right on the oven rack. At 325 degrees, they'll be tender in about one hour. Top with butter and sprinkle with cinnamon-sugar. It couldn't be easier!

Baked Ham in Peach Sauce

Doris Garner, Los Angeles, CA

Cornmeal Fried Catfish & Fresh Tartar Sauce

Serve these easy-to-prepare fillets with homemade tartar sauce or your favorite bottled cocktail sauce and hot sauce.

Makes 6 servings

3 large or 6 small catfish fillets
1/2 c. mustard
1 c. cornmeal
1 t. salt
1/2 t. pepper
2 T. oil
Garnish: lemon wedges

Rinse and dry fillets; brush with mustard. Combine cornmeal, salt and pepper in a large plastic zipping bag; shake bag to mix well. Pour oil into a skillet and place over medium-high heat. Add one fillet to bag and shake to coat. Add fillet to skillet, fry until golden on both sides and place in a brown paper bag to keep crisp. Repeat with remaining fillets, adding more oil, if needed. Serve with lemon wedges and Fresh Tartar Sauce.

Fresh Tartar Sauce:

1/2 c. sour cream
1/2 c. mayonnaise
1 t. lemon juice
2 T. onion, diced
1 T. fresh parsley, chopped

Combine all ingredients in a small bowl and mix well. Cover and refrigerate until chilled. Makes 1-1/4 cups.

★ GATHER 'ROUND ★ An old-fashioned fish fry is a terrific way to get together with family & friends. Usually held once a year in small towns, it has some of the best food around... crunchy fish, creamy coleslaw, homemade bread and a variety of desserts that can't be beat!

Cornmeal Fried Catfish & Fresh Tartar Sauce

Jackie Balla, Walbridge, OH

Barbecued Baby Back Ribs

Simmering the ribs first tenderizes them and removes excess fat. Serve with white bread and iced tea.

Makes 4 servings

2 T. olive oil
1 onion, chopped
1 stalk celery
1 clove garlic, minced
1 c. catsup
1/4 c. brown sugar, packed
1/4 c. red wine vinegar
2 T. Worcestershire sauce
1 T. Dijon mustard
3 lbs. baby back ribs

Heat oil in a saucepan over medium-high heat; add onion, celery and garlic. Sauté about 5 minutes, or until tender. Add all remaining ingredients except ribs; stir and simmer about 10 minutes. Place sauce in a food processor and process until smooth. Allow sauce to cool slightly. Bring a large stockpot of water to a boil; simmer ribs, covered, about 20 minutes. Drain ribs and dry with paper towels; baste generously with sauce. Grill over high heat 5 to 6 minutes on one side. Turn ribs and baste again. Grill 6 minutes longer.

Evelyn Russell, Dallas, TX

Mother's Fried Chicken

This recipe was given to me by my mother 30 years ago. It is always asked for when I cook for church get-togethers and Sunday dinners. The first time I made this for my pastor and his wife, it brought back memories for them of their mothers' fried chicken.

Makes 8 servings

4 c. self-rising flour
2 T. salt
2 T. coarsely ground pepper
8 lbs. chicken pieces
4 to 5 c. shortening, divided

Combine flour, salt and pepper in a shallow pan. Dredge chicken in flour mixture. In a large cast-iron skillet over medium-high heat, heat 3 cups shortening to 350 degrees. Working in batches, fry chicken, covered, about 10 minutes. Reduce heat to medium-low; fry 30 minutes per side. Add shortening as needed. Uncover during last 5 minutes of cooking time. Drain on paper towels.

★ HANDY TIP ★ For delicious, crispy golden fried chicken, be sure not to crowd the pan...use a large chicken fryer skillet or fry chicken in several batches.

Barbecued Baby Back Ribs

Amy Pierce, Flower Mound, TX

Black Bean Burgers

These burgers are very good...and they're healthy for you too. Served with all the fixin's, my kids don't even realize there is no meat inside!

Makes 8 servings

2 15-oz. cans black beans, drained
    and rinsed
2 onions, chopped
2 eggs, beaten
1 c. dry bread crumbs
1-1/2 t. garlic salt
2 t. cayenne pepper
8 whole-wheat buns, split
Garnish: sliced tomatoes, Swiss
    cheese slices

Place black beans and onion in a food processor; process until the mixture is mashed. Place bean mixture in a bowl; add eggs, bread crumbs, garlic salt and cayenne pepper and mix well. Shape into 8 patties. Cook on a grill or in a skillet over medium-high heat 5 minutes on each side, or until golden. Place burgers on buns; garnish with tomato and cheese slices.

Erin Gunn, Omaha, NE

Fajitas

These are always a favorite for casual dinner parties or when the whole family gets together...and the slow cooker does all the work!

Serves 8 to 10

1-1/2 lbs. beef round steak
14-1/2 oz. can diced tomatoes,
    drained
1 onion, sliced
1 green pepper, cut into strips
1 red pepper, cut into strips
1 jalapeño pepper, chopped
2 cloves garlic, minced
1 t. chili powder
1 t. ground cumin
1 t. ground coriander
1 t. fresh cilantro, chopped
1/4 t. salt
8 to 10 flour tortillas
Garnish: sour cream, guacamole,
    salsa, shredded cheese, shredded
    lettuce, fresh cilantro

Place beef in a 4-quart slow cooker. Combine remaining ingredients in a bowl, except tortillas and garnish; spoon over beef. Cover and cook on high setting for 4 to 5 hours or on low setting for 8 to 10 hours. Shred beef; stir into mixture in slow cooker. Serve with a slotted spoon on tortillas and garnish with favorite toppings.

Black Bean Burgers

Janet Bowlin, Fayetteville, AR

Louisiana Shrimp Boil

Just for fun, serve this meal with sliced French bread outdoors on a picnic table...and be sure to pass plenty of paper towels!

Makes 8 servings

4 onions, sliced
4 lemons, sliced
2 3-oz. pkgs. crab boil seasoning
Optional: hot pepper sauce to taste
32 new redskin potatoes
8 ears corn, husked and halved
4 lbs. uncooked medium shrimp in the shell

Fill 2 large stockpots half full with water; add onions, lemons, seasoning and hot pepper sauce, if using, to each stockpot. Bring water to a boil over medium-high heat; add potatoes and boil 10 minutes. Add corn; boil 5 minutes. Add shrimp; boil until shrimp turn pink and float to the surface. Drain; serve on a large platter.

Janet Bowlin, Fayetteville, AR

Slow-Cooker Sauerkraut Pork Roast

Just add mashed potatoes...everyone will beg for seconds!

Serves 6 to 8

3 to 4-lb. pork roast
1 T. oil
salt and pepper to taste
15-oz. can sauerkraut

Brown pork roast on all sides in oil in a skillet over high heat. Sprinkle with salt and pepper. Place roast in a 5-quart slow cooker; top with sauerkraut. Cover and cook on low setting for 6 to 8 hours.

★ PICNIC PERFECT ★ **Just for fun, serve an all-finger-food dinner. Serve Louisiana Shrimp Boil, French fries and fresh carrot and celery dippers with cups of creamy ranch dressing. For dessert, frosty fruit pops or ice cream sandwiches are perfect. Pass the napkins, please!**

Louisiana Shrimp Boil

Mary Kathryn Carter, Platte City, MO

Cream Cheese Enchiladas

This creamy variation on Mexican enchiladas is yummy! It won me first place in a local newspaper's holiday cooking contest.

Makes 8 servings

2 8-oz. pkgs. cream cheese, softened
1 c. sour cream
2 10-oz. cans mild green chile enchilada sauce
1/4 c. jalapeño peppers, seeded and chopped
1 lb. ground beef, browned and drained
1/2 c. shredded sharp Cheddar cheese
8 to 12 flour tortillas
1 sweet onion, chopped
1/2 c. sliced black olives
Garnish: sliced black olives, chopped tomato, shredded lettuce, chopped green onions, salsa, shredded cheese

In a large bowl, blend together cream cheese, sour cream, enchilada sauce and jalapeños; set aside. Combine ground beef and shredded cheese in another bowl; set aside. Fill each tortilla with one to 2 tablespoons cream cheese mixture and one to 2 tablespoons beef mixture. Sprinkle each with onion and olives; roll up tortillas. Place seam-side down in an ungreased 13"x9" baking pan; cover with remaining cream cheese mixture. Bake, uncovered, at 400 degrees for 30 to 40 minutes; cover if top begins to brown. Garnish as desired.

★ MAKE IT A PARTY ★ Visit a party supply store for festive sombreros...turn them upside-down, fill with tortilla chips and serve alongside Cream Cheese Enchiladas. Olé!

Cream Cheese Enchiladas

Jerry Lyttle, St. Clair Shores, MI

Beef Fajita Skewers

Serve with warmed flour tortillas, sour cream and salsa...a clever new way to enjoy a Mexican restaurant favorite.

Makes 8 servings

2 lbs. boneless beef top sirloin,
   sliced into 1-inch cubes
16 wooden skewers, soaked in water
2 green peppers, cut into wedges
2 red or yellow peppers, cut into
   wedges
4 onions, cut into wedges
6 T. lime juice
3/4 c. Italian salad dressing
salt to taste

Thread beef cubes onto 8 skewers; thread peppers and onions onto remaining skewers. Combine lime juice and salad dressing; brush over skewers. Grill over hot coals or on a medium-hot grill, turning occasionally, 7 to 9 minutes for beef and 12 to 15 minutes for vegetables. Sprinkle with salt to taste.

Wendy Jacobs, Idaho Falls, ID

Preference Dinner

While in college, there was a yearly dance called Preference. At the dance, the ladies invited the men and prepared a dinner for them. This was the dinner I prepared for my date. My cooking must not have been too bad...we've been married now for many years.

Makes 6 servings

3 T. lime juice
1/4 t. salt
1 t. pepper
1-1/4 lb. beef flank steak
2 c. broccoli flowerets
2 c. baby carrots, sliced
2 ears corn, husked and cut into
   2-inch pieces
1 red onion, sliced into wedges
1 T. olive oil

Combine lime juice, salt and pepper; brush over both sides of steak. Place on a broiler pan and broil, 5 minutes per side, turning once. Set aside on a cutting board; keep warm. Toss broccoli, carrots, corn and onion with oil. Spoon onto a lightly greased baking sheet in a single layer. Bake at 475 degrees, turning once, until cooked through, about 10 minutes. Slice steak into thin strips and arrange on a platter. Surround with vegetables.

Beef Fajita Skewers

Nancy Wise, Little Rock, AR

Buttermilk Fried Chicken

This is pure, down-home goodness... delicious warm from the skillet or wrapped in wax paper to savor cold as a picnic lunch with coleslaw.

Makes 6 servings

1 c. buttermilk
3-1/2 lbs. chicken, cut up
1 c. plus 3 T. all-purpose flour, divided
1-1/2 t. salt
1/2 t. pepper
oil for frying
1 c. milk
1-1/2 c. water
salt and pepper to taste

Pour buttermilk over chicken pieces in a large shallow dish; cover and refrigerate one hour. Combine one cup flour, salt and pepper in a large plastic zipping bag. Drain chicken and add to bag, one piece at a time, shaking to coat. Place on wax paper; let stand 15 minutes. Heat 1/4 inch oil in a large cast-iron skillet over medium heat. Add chicken; cook until golden on all sides. Reduce heat to low; cover and simmer 25 to 30 minutes, until juices run clear when chicken is pierced. Uncover; cook, turning often, an additional 5 minutes. Drain chicken on paper towels; keep warm. For gravy, pour off all except 1/4 cup drippings from skillet. Stir in remaining flour over low heat until well blended; gradually add milk. Slowly stir in water; bring to a boil over medium heat. Cook 2 minutes, or until thickened, stirring constantly. Add salt and pepper to taste. Serve gravy with chicken.

★ HOT TIP ★ Keep color and texture contrasts in mind as you plan dinner. For example, crispy, golden fried chicken teamed with creamy white macaroni salad and juicy red tomato slices...everything will taste twice as good!

Buttermilk Fried Chicken

Holly Higgins, Arnold, MD

Golden Crab Cakes

Mix up some fresh tartar sauce! Add a tablespoon each of minced onion and pickle relish to a cup of mayonnaise and chill.

Makes 8 servings

3 c. saltine crackers, crushed and
   divided
2 eggs, beaten
1/2 c. onion, diced
3 T. mayonnaise
1 T. mustard
2 t. lemon juice
1/2 t. salt
1/4 t. pepper
1/8 t. cayenne pepper
1/4 t. hot pepper sauce
1 lb. refrigerated fresh lump
   crabmeat
2 T. butter
2 T. oil
Garnish: tartar sauce

Stir together 2 cups cracker crumbs, eggs, onion, mayonnaise, mustard, lemon juice and seasonings. Fold in crabmeat. Shape into eight, 3-inch patties; dredge in remaining crumbs. Melt butter and oil together in a skillet over medium-high heat. Cook crab cakes until golden, about 4 minutes on each side. Serve with tartar sauce.

Shari Miller, Hobart, IN

Cheeseburger & Fries Casserole

The recipe name says it all...kids will love it!

Serves 6 to 8

2 lbs. ground beef, browned and
   drained
10-3/4 oz. can golden mushroom
   soup
10-3/4 oz. can Cheddar cheese soup
16-oz. pkg. frozen crinkle-cut
   French fries
Garnish: chopped tomato, chopped
   dill pickle

Combine beef and soups; spread mixture in a greased 13"x9" baking pan. Arrange French fries on top. Bake, uncovered, at 350 degrees for 50 to 55 minutes, until fries are golden. Garnish with chopped tomato and dill pickle.

Golden Crab Cakes

Stephanie Moon, Nampa, ID

Ham & Pineapple Kabobs

Soak wooden kabob skewers in water at least 20 minutes before using...they won't burn or stick.

Serves 8 to 10

2 lbs. smoked ham, cut into
   1-inch cubes
2 8-oz. cans pineapple chunks,
   drained and juice reserved
8 to 10 skewers, soaked in water
1/4 c. soy sauce
1/4 c. brown sugar, packed
1/4 t. ground ginger

Thread ham cubes and pineapple chunks on skewers; place in an ungreased 2-quart casserole dish. Combine reserved juice and remaining ingredients; pour over kabobs, turning to coat. Cover and refrigerate for 2 hours, turning occasionally. Grill over medium-hot coals, turning twice and brushing with marinade until hot and golden, about 10 minutes.

Dueley Lucas, Somerset, KY

Chicken & Dressing Bake

Such a comforting dinner, and so easy to make!

Makes 8 servings

2 6-oz. pkgs. cornbread stuffing mix
1 t. dried sage
1/4 t. pepper
1 onion, finely chopped
4 stalks celery, finely chopped
2 10-3/4 oz. cans cream of chicken
   soup
2 c. chicken broth
2 c. shredded Cheddar cheese,
   divided
4 boneless, skinless chicken breasts,
   cooked and cut in half lengthwise

In a large bowl, combine stuffing mix, sage and pepper. Add onion and celery. Add soup, broth and one cup cheese to stuffing mixture; mix well. Place stuffing mixture in a 13"x9" baking pan that has been sprayed with non-stick vegetable spray. Place chicken on top of stuffing mixture. Top with remaining cheese. Cover and bake at 350 degrees for 30 minutes.

Ham & Pineapple Kabobs

Carrie O'Shea, Marina Del Rey, CA

Rosemary Pork Loin

I grow rosemary in my garden, so I'm always looking for recipes to use it in. I've tried many chicken dishes, but I had never paired pork and rosemary until my sister shared this recipe with me. Yum!

Makes 8 servings

2 T. butter
2 1-lb. pork tenderloins
salt and pepper to taste
2 c. sliced mushrooms
1/4 c. onion, finely chopped
3 T. fresh rosemary, chopped
2 cloves garlic, minced
2 T. cooking sherry or apple juice
Garnish: fresh rosemary sprigs

Melt butter in a heavy skillet over medium-high heat. Sprinkle pork tenderloins with salt and pepper to taste. Brown pork quickly in butter, about one minute on each side. Remove pork to an ungreased roasting pan, reserving drippings in skillet. Bake pork at 350 degrees for 20 to 25 minutes, until a thermometer registers 145 degrees. Let stand 5 minutes before slicing and placing on a platter. Add remaining ingredients (except sherry or juice and garnish) to skillet. Cook and stir over low heat several minutes, or until mushrooms and onion are almost tender. Stir in sherry or juice. Spoon mushroom mixture over pork slices. Garnish with rosemary.

★ BROWN IT UP ★ Pork chops will brown better if patted dry first with a paper towel.

Rosemary Pork Loin

Stephanie McNealy, Talala, OK

Family-Favorite Chili Mac

Kids love this quick & easy dinner. Serve with a tossed salad and cornbread sticks.

Makes 8 servings

2 7-1/4 oz. pkgs. macaroni & cheese, uncooked
10-oz. can diced tomatoes with green chiles
1 to 2 lbs. ground beef
1-1/4 oz. pkg. taco seasoning mix
chili powder to taste
salt and pepper to taste

Prepare macaroni & cheese according to package directions. Stir in tomatoes with green chiles; set aside. Brown ground beef in a skillet over medium-high heat; drain and mix in taco seasoning. Stir beef mixture into macaroni mixture. Add seasonings as desired; heat through.

Betty Charles, Dayton, OH

Enchilada-Stuffed Poblanos

Mexican food hot off the grill! Serve with cheesy rice and tortilla chips for a delicious meal.

Makes 6 servings

2-1/2 c. cooked chicken, shredded
15-oz. can black beans, drained and rinsed
11-oz. can corn, drained
10-oz. can diced tomatoes with green chiles, drained
10-oz. can enchilada sauce
1 t. salt
2 c. shredded Mexican-blend cheese, divided
6 poblano peppers, halved lengthwise and seeded

In a large bowl, combine chicken, beans, corn, tomatoes, enchilada sauce, salt and 1-1/2 cups cheese. Fill pepper halves evenly with chicken mixture. Wrap each half loosely in aluminum foil. Grill over medium-high heat for about 20 minutes, until heated through and peppers are tender. Unwrap; sprinkle with remaining cheese and let stand several minutes, until cheese is melted.

★ SIMPLE SIDE ★ Delicious alongside any Mexican dish, try this sweet-hot butter for spreading over homemade cornbread. Blend together one cup softened butter with 1/4 cup maple syrup and 1/2 teaspoon Mexican hot pepper sauce.

Family-Favorite Chili Mac

MAINS & BURGERS

Angela Murphy, Tempe, AZ

Make-Ahead Chicken Chile Rolls

Make this scrumptious casserole the night before, refrigerate it overnight and pop it in the oven the next evening...what a timesaver!

Makes 8 servings

8 boneless, skinless chicken breasts
1/3 lb. Monterey Jack cheese, cut into 6 strips
7-oz. can diced green chiles
3/4 c. dry bread crumbs
3/4 c. grated Parmesan cheese
1 T. chili powder
1/2 t. salt
1/4 t. pepper
1/4 t. ground cumin
1/2 c. butter, melted
2-1/2 c. enchilada sauce
Garnish: shredded Mexican blend cheese, diced tomatoes, chopped green onions

Flatten chicken breasts to 1/4-inch thickness between pieces of wax paper. Top each piece of chicken with one strip of cheese and 2 tablespoons chiles; roll up. Combine bread crumbs, Parmesan cheese and seasonings in a bowl; place melted butter in a separate bowl. Dip chicken rolls in butter and coat in crumb mixture. Arrange chicken rolls in a lightly greased 13"x9" baking pan, seam-side down; drizzle with any remaining butter. Cover and chill overnight. The next day, uncover and bake at 400 degrees for 30 minutes, or until heated through. Shortly before serving time, warm enchilada sauce in a saucepan or in the microwave; ladle sauce evenly over chicken. Garnish as desired.

★ MAKE AHEAD ★ For easy make-ahead, super-simple cheese snacks, cut several 8-ounce packages of cream cheese into 10 cubes each. Shape cubes into balls and roll in snipped fresh parsley or chopped pecans. Just arrange on a plate, cover and pop in the fridge until party time.

120 Our Best Family Recipes

Make-Ahead Chicken Chile Rolls

Stacie Avner, Delaware, OH

Mexican Burgers

Chili powder, cumin and Pepper Jack cheese add a little zip to these tasty burgers.

Makes 5 servings

1 avocado, peeled, pitted and diced
1 plum tomato, diced
2 green onions, chopped
1 to 2 t. lime juice
1-1/4 lbs. ground beef
1 egg, beaten
3/4 c. to 1 c. nacho-flavored tortilla
   chips, crushed
1/4 c. fresh cilantro, chopped
1/2 t. chili powder
1/2 t. ground cumin
salt and pepper to taste
1-1/4 c. shredded Pepper Jack cheese
5 hamburger buns, split

Combine avocado, tomato, onions and lime juice; mash slightly and set aside. Combine ground beef, egg, chips and seasonings in a large bowl. Form into 5 patties; grill over medium-high heat to desired doneness, turning to cook on both sides. Sprinkle cheese over burgers; grill until melted. Place burgers on bottoms of buns; top with avocado mixture and bun tops.

Brandi Glenn, Los Osos, CA

Gobblin' Good Turkey Burgers

This was my mom's recipe...I'll take these over plain old hamburgers any day!

Makes 4 to 6 servings

1 lb. ground turkey
1 onion, minced
1 c. shredded Cheddar cheese
1/4 c. Worcestershire sauce
1/2 t. dry mustard
salt and pepper to taste
4 to 6 hamburger buns, split

Combine all ingredients except buns in a large bowl and mix well; shape mixture into 4 to 6 patties. Grill over medium-high heat until cooked through and center registers 165 degrees on a meat thermometer. Serve on hamburger buns.

★ SAVVY TIP ★ For the juiciest burgers, flip grilled burgers with a spatula, not a fork. The holes a fork makes will let the juices escape.

Mexican Burgers

Jennie Gist, Gooseberry Patch

Shrimp Kabobs

This recipe is easy to double or triple for a crowd!

Makes 4 servings

3 carrots, peeled and cut diagonally
1 green pepper, cut into 1-inch
    strips
1/4 c. water
1/2 t. orange zest
1/2 c. orange juice
2 t. fresh thyme, minced
2 t. canola oil
12 to 16 uncooked large shrimp,
    peeled and cleaned

Combine carrots, green pepper and water in a saucepan. Bring to a boil, cover and simmer 3 minutes. In a small bowl, combine orange zest, orange juice, thyme and oil. Set aside. Lightly grease grill or broiler pan. Thread shrimp, carrots and peppers on skewers; place on grill. Baste kabobs with orange juice mixture and grill 3 inches from heat for 2 minutes. Turn kabobs, baste and grill another 3 minutes, or until shrimp turn pink.

Maureen Day, Marion, OH

Super-Easy BBQ Chicken

Perfect for a rainy-day meal! So simple to fix in your slow cooker...just add a fresh green salad.

Serves 6 to 8

16 chicken drumsticks and/or thighs,
    skin removed
2 c. favorite barbecue sauce
cooked rice

Place chicken in a microwave-safe dish. Cover and microwave on high for 15 minutes. Carefully remove hot chicken to a 6-quart slow cooker, spooning some barbecue sauce over each piece. Cover and cook on low setting for 6 to 8 hours, until chicken is very tender. Discard bones. Serve chicken and sauce over cooked rice.

★ SNACK ATTACK ★ Munch on kabobs after school...skewer fresh veggies and cubes of cheese on toothpicks and make snack time more fun!

Shrimp Kabobs

Feta Beans, Page 132

CHAPTER FOUR

Casseroles, Sides & Salads

Hazel's Stuffing Balls, Page 140

Veggie-Chicken Bake, Page 152

Cindy Jamieson, Ontario, Canada

Brown Sugar-Bacon Squash

I fell in love with this recipe while working at a restaurant with my friend. A few months later, we started dating and have been together for ten years. It's one of the few ways I like to eat squash. By the way, here in Ontario we call them pepper squash!

Makes 8 servings

1 acorn squash, peeled, halved and
  seeds removed
1/3 c. butter
salt and pepper to taste
1 c. brown sugar, packed
8 slices bacon, halved

Cut each squash half into quarters and cut each quarter in half, to create 16 pieces. Place squash skin-side down on an aluminum foil-lined rimmed baking sheet. Top each piece with one teaspoon butter, salt, pepper, one tablespoon brown sugar and 1/2 slice bacon. Bake, uncovered, at 350 degrees for 30 to 45 minutes, until bacon is crisp and squash is tender.

Paula Smith, Ottawa, IL

Quick & Easy Parmesan Asparagus

From oven to table in only 15 minutes!

Serves 8 to 10

4 lbs. asparagus, trimmed
1/4 c. butter, melted
2 c. shredded Parmesan cheese
1 t. salt
1/2 t. pepper

Place asparagus and one inch of water in a large skillet. Bring to a boil. Reduce heat; cover and simmer 5 to 7 minutes, until crisp-tender. Drain and arrange asparagus in a greased 13"x9" baking pan. Drizzle with butter; sprinkle with Parmesan cheese, salt and pepper. Bake, uncovered, at 350 degrees for 10 to 15 minutes, until cheese is melted.

★ DOUBLE DUTY ★ Scoop out the inside of an acorn squash and use it as a serving bowl for creamy chicken or tuna salad.

Brown Sugar-Bacon Squash

Sandra Manchester, Cedar Rapid, IA

Crunchy Granny Smith Salad

Crisp Granny Smith apples make this salad especially refreshing.

Serves 10 to 12

1 head leaf lettuce, torn, washed
    and pat dry
2 Granny Smith apples, cored, sliced
    and cut in half
1 c. shredded Swiss cheese
1 c. cashews, chopped
1 c. oil
1 T. onion, minced
1 t. dry mustard
1/2 c. sugar
1/3 c. cider vinegar
2 t. poppy seed

Layer the first 4 ingredients in a bowl. Combine the next 5 ingredients in a blender; process until smooth. Add poppy seed; pulse 2 times. Pour desired amount of dressing over salad.

Tom Griffith, Grand Junction, CO

Scallops & Shrimp with Linguine

Everyone will love this!

Makes 8 servings

3 T. butter, divided
3 T. olive oil, divided
1 lb. uncooked large shrimp, peeled
    and cleaned
3 cloves garlic, minced and divided
1 lb. uncooked fresh sea scallops
8-oz. pkg. sliced mushrooms
2 c. snow peas, trimmed
2 tomatoes, chopped
1/2 c. green onion, chopped
1 t. salt
1/2 t. red pepper flakes
1/4 c. fresh parsley, chopped
2 T. fresh basil, chopped
10-oz. pkg. linguine pasta, cooked
    and kept warm
Garnish: grated Parmesan cheese

Heat one tablespoon each of butter and olive oil in a large skillet over medium-high heat. Add shrimp and half of garlic; cook 2 to 3 minutes or until shrimp turn pink. Remove shrimp from skillet; keep warm. Repeat procedure with scallops. Heat remaining butter and oil in same skillet over medium heat. Add mushrooms, snow peas, tomatoes, green onion, salt, pepper, parsley and basil; cook 4 to 5 minutes. In a large bowl, combine linguine, mushroom mixture, shrimp and scallops; toss well. Serve with Parmesan cheese.

Crunchy Granny Smith Salad

Cyndy DeStefano, Mercer, PA

Feta Beans

This is such a great side dish. You can use canned or frozen green beans, but it is especially good with green beans right from the garden!

Serves 8 to 10

16-oz. pkg. frozen green beans
1/4 c. butter
16-oz. pkg. sliced mushrooms
1 onion, finely diced
2 cloves garlic, minced
1 t. salt
1/2 t. pepper
4-oz. container crumbled feta cheese

Prepare green beans according to package directions; drain. Melt butter in a large skillet over medium heat. Add mushrooms, onion, garlic, salt and pepper. Cook 5 to 7 minutes, until heated through. Stir in beans and cheese. Serve immediately.

Jo Ann, Gooseberry Patch

Mandarin Orange Salad

Quick & easy to prepare, this salad is best topped with a fresh dressing like Raspberry Vinaigrette.

Makes 8 servings

8 c. green or red loose-leaf lettuce,
    torn into bite-size pieces
3 15-oz. cans mandarin oranges,
    drained
1 c. walnut pieces, toasted
1 red onion, sliced

Combine all ingredients together. Toss with desired amount of Raspberry Vinaigrette and serve.

Raspberry Vinaigrette:

2/3 c. raspberry vinegar
2/3 c. seedless raspberry jam
1-1/2 t. dried ground coriander
    or cumin
3/4 t. salt
1/2 t. pepper
1-1/2 c. olive oil

Combine first 5 ingredients in blender. Turn blender on high, gradually adding oil. Chill.

Feta Beans

Sandy Coffey, Cincinnati, OH

Game Board Night Casserole

Whenever we have family over to play board games, this recipe is super easy and super good. Serve with warm rolls and celery sticks. Now let the games begin!

Makes 8 servings

10-3/4 oz. can cream of chicken or celery soup
1/2 c. mayonnaise
1/2 c. milk
garlic powder, salt and pepper to taste
2 c. cooked chicken, cubed
1/2 c. carrot, peeled and grated
20-oz. pkg. frozen diced hashbrown potatoes
1 c. canned cut green beans, drained
3/4 c. shredded Cheddar cheese
1/2 c. seasoned dry bread crumbs

In a large bowl, stir together soup, mayonnaise, milk and seasonings. Stir in chicken, carrot, potatoes and beans. Transfer to a lightly greased 13"x9" baking pan. Sprinkle cheese and bread crumbs on top. Bake, uncovered, at 400 degrees for 40 minutes, or until hot and bubbly.

Beth Bundy, Long Prairie, MN

Crowd-Size Pizza Hot Dish

This dish is perfect to make one for dinner, and freeze one for later!

Makes 2 pans, each serves 15

6 c. elbow macaroni, uncooked
3 lbs. ground beef
1 onion, chopped
3 15-oz. cans tomato sauce
1-1/2 T. salt
1 T. pepper
1 T. dried oregano
2 t. garlic powder
3 eggs, beaten
1-1/2 c. milk
2 16-oz. pkgs. shredded Cheddar cheese

Cook macaroni according to package directions; drain. Place in a large bowl and set aside. In a skillet over medium heat, brown beef and onion together; drain. Stir in tomato sauce and seasonings; blend well. Simmer for 5 to 10 minutes, stirring occasionally. Whisk eggs and milk together; blend into macaroni. Add beef mixture and stir well. Transfer into 2 greased 13"x9" baking pans. Top with cheese. Bake, uncovered, at 350 degrees for 20 minutes, or until heated through. Let stand 10 minutes before cutting.

Game Board Night Casserole

Melissa Garland, Annville, PA

Baked Corn

A delicious side dish for everyday
dinners and holiday buffets!

Makes 12 servings

2 eggs, beaten
1 c. sour cream
15-oz. can creamed corn
15-1/4 oz. can corn
7-oz. pkg. corn muffin mix
1/2 c. butter, softened

Combine eggs and sour cream in a
large bowl; add creamed corn and corn,
mixing well. Stir in muffin mix; add
butter. Pour into a lightly greased
8"x8" baking pan. Bake, uncovered,
at 350 degrees for 35 to 45 minutes.

Sherri Cooper, Armada, MI

Skillet-Toasted Corn Salad

Whenever my father comes to visit,
this salad is one that he requests.
He usually stops by the local
farmers' vegetable stand on his way
to our house and picks up fresh ears
of corn...just for this salad!

Serves 6 to 8

1/3 c. plus 1 T. olive oil, divided
1/3 c. lemon juice
1 T. Worcestershire sauce
3 cloves garlic, minced
3 to 4 dashes hot pepper sauce
1/4 t. salt
1/2 t. pepper
6 ears sweet corn, husks and
    kernels removed
4 red, yellow and green
    peppers, coarsely chopped
1/2 c. grated Parmesan cheese
1 head romaine lettuce, cut
    crosswise into 1-inch pieces

Combine 1/3 cup oil, lemon juice,
Worcestershire sauce, garlic, hot
pepper sauce, salt and pepper in
a jar with a tight-fitting lid. Cover
and shake well; set aside. Heat
remaining oil in a large skillet over
medium-high heat. Add corn kernels;
sauté 5 minutes, or until corn is
tender and golden, stirring often.
Remove from heat. Combine corn,
peppers and cheese in a large bowl.
Pour dressing over corn mixture; toss
lightly to coat. Serve over lettuce.

Baked Corn

Carole Griffin, Mount Vernon, OH

Grandma Lucy's Corn Fritters

Showcase the bounty of summer corn with a batch of these delicately fried fritters. When sweet corn is not at its peak, substitute 3 cups of canned or frozen corn kernels.

Makes one dozen

4 ears sweet corn, cooked
2 eggs, beaten
1/4 c. milk
1/2 c. all-purpose flour
1 t. baking powder
1 t. sugar
1/2 t. salt
1 t. bacon drippings or oil
Optional: butter, maple syrup

Cut kernels from corn and place in a medium mixing bowl; stir in eggs and milk. Combine flour, baking powder, sugar and salt in a small bowl; stir into corn mixture, mixing gently. Heat bacon drippings or oil in a skillet over medium-high heat. Drop batter by 1/4 cupfuls into skillet and cook until lightly browned, flipping to brown the other side. Serve with butter and maple syrup, if desired.

Elizabeth Burkhalter, Oshkosh, WI

Company's Coming Fruit Salad

Try canned peaches or pears in this recipe, too...both are delicious!

Makes 12 servings

8-oz. pkg. cream cheese, softened
3/4 c. sugar
10-oz. pkg. frozen sliced
    strawberries, thawed and drained
2 bananas, sliced
10-oz. container frozen whipped
    topping, thawed
8-oz. can crushed pineapple, drained
1 c. sweetened flaked coconut
1 c. chopped pecans

In a large bowl, beat together cream cheese and sugar with an electric mixer on medium speed. Fold in remaining ingredients by hand. Spread in a 13"x9" baking pan. Cover and freeze 3 to 4 hours, until firm. Remove from freezer a few minutes before serving time; cut into squares.

Grandma Lucy's Corn Fritters

Andrea Barclay, Somerset, PA

Hazel's Stuffing Balls

My mother-in-law gave me this recipe when I hosted my first Thanksgiving dinner. This is also wonderful with chicken and roast pork loin dinners. Nowadays I usually double the recipe... you can't have too many stuffing balls!

Makes 12 servings

1-1/2 to 2 loaves white bread, torn into pieces
1/2 c. butter
1-1/2 to 2 c. celery, finely chopped
Optional: 1/2 c. onion, chopped
1-1/2 t. salt
1-1/2 t. pepper
1/2 t. poultry seasoning
1 to 2 t. dried parsley
6 eggs, beaten
1/4 to 1/2 c. turkey or chicken broth

The night before, place bread pieces on a baking sheet or in a large bowl to dry. The next day, melt butter in a skillet over medium-low heat. Sauté celery and onion, if using, for 15 to 20 minutes; cool slightly. In a very large bowl, toss bread pieces and seasonings with butter mixture. Add eggs and just enough broth to help mixture to stick together; mix well. Form into 12 balls; place in a 13"x9" baking pan sprayed with non-stick vegetable spray. Drizzle a little more broth over stuffing balls; cover with aluminum foil. Bake at 350 degrees for 20 to 30 minutes, uncovering for the last few minutes, until balls are crisp and golden.

★ SAVVY SWITCH ★ Turn leftover Stuffing Balls into a tasty main dish by tossing in some browned sausage. Simply spoon crumbled stuffing into green peppers or squash halves and bake at 350 degrees until heated through and tender.

Hazel's Stuffing Balls

Aimee Bowlin, Keithville, LA

Creamy Chicken Spaghetti

This is one of my husband's favorite meals, and I enjoy making it because it's so quick & easy!

Makes 8 servings

2 lbs. chicken breasts, cooked
   and shredded
16-oz. pkg. spaghetti, cooked
2 14-1/2 oz. cans stewed
   tomatoes, chopped
2 10-3/4 oz. cans cream of
   chicken soup
10-3/4 oz. can cream of mushroom
   soup
8-oz. pkg. pasteurized process
   cheese spread, cubed
4-oz. can sliced mushrooms, drained

Combine all ingredients in a Dutch oven; cook over medium heat until warmed through and cheese is melted.

Jennifer Clingan, Dayton, OH

Pizza Pasta

Add in some banana peppers for a little kick if you like!

Makes 8 servings

1 lb. ground Italian pork sausage
1 c. onion, chopped
8-oz. pkg. rotini pasta, cooked
8-oz. pkg. sliced mushrooms
4-oz. pkg. sliced pepperoni
15-oz. can pizza sauce
1/2 green pepper, chopped
2-1/4 oz. can sliced black olives,
   drained
8-oz. pkg. shredded mozzarella
   cheese

Brown sausage and onion in a skillet over medium heat; drain and transfer to an ungreased 3-quart casserole dish. Set aside. Combine pasta, mushrooms, pepperoni, pizza sauce, pepper and olives in a large bowl; spoon over sausage. Sprinkle with cheese; cover and bake at 350 degrees for 45 minutes. Uncover and bake an additional 5 to 10 minutes.

Creamy Chicken Spaghetti

Sheila Collier, Kingwood, TX

Cajun Seafood Fettuccine

So good, sometimes this only serves four!

Makes 8 servings

1/2 c. butter, divided
2 8-oz. pkgs. frozen seasoned
   vegetable blend
garlic powder and Cajun seasoning
   to taste
1/4 c. water
1/4 c. all-purpose flour
1 pt. half-and-half
16-oz. pkg. pasteurized processed
   cheese spread, cubed
1-1/2 lbs. medium shrimp, peeled
   and cleaned
1-1/2 lbs. crabmeat, flaked or chopped
12-oz. pkg. egg noodles, cooked
12-oz. pkg. shredded Colby Jack
   cheese
Garnish: fresh parsley, chopped

Melt 1/4 cup butter in a large saucepan; add vegetables and sauté until tender. Sprinkle with garlic powder and Cajun seasoning; set aside. Add water to flour to make a thick paste that is still able to be poured; add to skillet. Stir in half-and-half and cheese spread; continue stirring until cheese is melted. Set aside. Sauté shrimp in remaining butter in a separate skillet until no longer pink. Add shrimp and crabmeat to vegetable mixture and let simmer on medium-low heat for 20 minutes. Stir in egg noodles; pour into an ungreased 13"x9" baking pan. Sprinkle with Colby Jack cheese. Bake, uncovered, at 350 degrees for 20 minutes. Garnish with parsley.

★ JUST FOR FUN ★ Shake up a recipe for a change of pace. Use angel hair pasta in main dishes or try rotini or wagon wheel pasta in salads.

Cajun Seafood Fettuccine

Chris Revennaugh, Mentor, OH

Candied Sweet Potatoes

We love this clever way to fix an old favorite by using an oven roasting bag. There's no messy, sticky clean-up... just toss away the bag!

Serves 6 to 8

1/4 c. all-purpose flour
4 sweet potatoes, peeled and thinly
   sliced
1/3 c. brown sugar, packed
1/4 c. margarine, sliced
2 T. maple-flavored pancake syrup
1/4 t. nutmeg

Shake flour in a large oven bag; arrange bag in a 13"x9" baking pan. Toss sweet potatoes with remaining ingredients to blend; arrange in an even layer inside bag. Close bag with provided nylon tie; cut six 1/2-inch slits in top. Bake at 350 degrees for 45 minutes.

Annette Ingram, Grand Rapids, MI

Squash Casserole

For a spicier dish, use hot sausage.

Makes 8 servings

1/2 lb. ground pork sausage
3 zucchini, sliced
1 onion, finely chopped
2 T. butter
2 8-3/4 oz. cans cream-style corn
2 c. shredded Monterey Jack cheese
3/4 c. cornbread stuffing
4-1/2 oz. can chopped green chiles,
   drained

Brown sausage in a skillet, stirring until it crumbles; drain well and set aside. In a large skillet over medium heat, sauté zucchini and onion in butter until tender. Combine zucchini mixture, sausage, corn, cheese, stuffing and chiles; stir well. Spoon into a lightly greased 2-quart casserole dish. Bake, uncovered, at 350 degrees for 40 minutes, or until golden and bubbly.

★ SNACK ATTACK ★ Sweet potato chips...a delicious snack! Peel sweet potatoes, slice thinly and toss with oil. Bake on a baking sheet at 400 degrees for 22 to 25 minutes, turning once. Sprinkle with cinnamon-sugar and serve warm.

Candied Sweet Potatoes

Annette Martinelli, New York, NY

Italian Zucchini Casserole

Even kids like this side dish! Makes a delicious meatless meal too.

Serves 6 to 8

3 zucchini, sliced
3 T. olive oil, divided
1 onion, sliced
1 clove garlic, minced
28-oz. can diced tomatoes
1 T. fresh basil, minced
1-1/2 t. fresh oregano, minced
1/2 t. garlic salt
1/4 t. pepper
1-1/2 c. favorite-flavor stuffing mix
1/2 c. grated Parmesan cheese
3/4 c. shredded mozzarella cheese

Cook zucchini in one tablespoon oil in a skillet over medium heat for 5 to 6 minutes, until tender. Drain and remove from skillet. Sauté onion and garlic in remaining oil for one minute. Add tomatoes, basil, oregano, salt and pepper; simmer, uncovered, for 10 minutes. Remove from heat; gently stir in zucchini. Place in an ungreased 13"x9" baking pan. Top with stuffing mix; sprinkle with Parmesan cheese. Cover and bake at 350 degrees for 20 minutes. Uncover and sprinkle with mozzarella cheese. Bake for 10 more minutes, or until cheese is bubbly and golden.

★ FREEZE IT ★ Too many zucchini from your garden? Grate extra zucchini and freeze it in two-cup portions...it'll be ready to add to your favorite recipes all winter long.

Italian Zucchini Casserole

Cindy McPeak, Ithaca, NY

Party Paella Casserole

Here's a great use for rotisserie chicken, shrimp and yellow rice.

Makes 8 servings

2 8-oz. pkgs. yellow rice, uncooked
1 lb. medium shrimp, peeled and
  cleaned
1 T. fresh lemon juice
1/2 t. salt
1/4 t. pepper
2 cloves garlic, minced
1-1/2 T. olive oil
2-1/2 lb. lemon-and-garlic deli
  roast chicken, boned and
  coarsely shredded
5 green onions, chopped
8-oz. container sour cream
1 c. frozen English peas, thawed
1 c. green olives with pimentos,
  coarsely chopped
1-1/2 c. shredded Monterey Jack
  cheese
1/2 t. smoked Spanish paprika

Prepare rice according to package directions. Remove from heat and let cool 30 minutes; fluff with a fork. Meanwhile, toss shrimp with lemon juice, salt and pepper in a bowl. Sauté shrimp and garlic in hot oil in a large non-stick skillet 2 minutes, or just until done. Remove from heat. Combine shredded chicken, cooked rice, onions, sour cream and peas in a large bowl; toss well. Add shrimp and olives, tossing gently. Spoon rice mixture into a greased 13"x9" baking pan. Combine cheese and paprika, tossing well; sprinkle over casserole. Bake, uncovered, at 400 degrees for 15 minutes, or just until cheese is melted and casserole is thoroughly heated.

★ TOP IT OFF ★ A new twist on casserole toppers...try crushed veggie, chicken or cheese-flavored crackers combined with fresh or dried herbs and melted butter. Sprinkle on top before baking for a delicious crunch.

Party Paella Casserole

Theresa Currie, Chatham, NJ

Veggie-Chicken Bake

A quick-to-fix dish that's rich & creamy.

Serves 6 to 8

4 boneless, skinless chicken
    breasts, cooked and diced
1 c. mayonnaise
1 c. shredded Cheddar cheese
2 10-3/4 oz. cans cream of chicken
    soup
16-oz. pkg. frozen broccoli and
    cauliflower, thawed and drained
12-oz. pkg. egg noodles, cooked

Combine chicken, mayonnaise, cheese, soup and vegetables. Spoon into an ungreased 13"x9" baking pan. Bake, uncovered, at 350 degrees for about 45 minutes, until heated through. Serve over noodles.

Karen Holder, Hamilton, OH

Tomato-Corn Casserole

For a leaner version, try substituting ground turkey for the ground beef.

Serves 10 to 12

1 onion, chopped
1 green pepper, chopped
1 T. olive oil
2 lbs. ground beef
16-oz. pkg. medium egg noodles,
    cooked
14-3/4 oz. can creamed corn
15-oz. can tomato sauce
1 T. cocktail sauce
1 c. shredded Cheddar cheese

Sauté onion and green pepper in oil in a 10" skillet over medium-high heat until tender. Add beef to skillet and cook until browned; remove skillet from heat and drain. Stir in cooked noodles, corn, tomato sauce and cocktail sauce; spoon into a lightly greased 13"x9" baking pan. Bake, uncovered, at 350 degrees for 25 minutes; sprinkle with cheese and bake until cheese melts. Serve warm.

★ QUICK TIP ★ A no-fuss way to cook egg noodles...bring water to a rolling boil, then turn off heat. Add noodles; cover and let stand for 20 minutes, stirring twice. Perfect!

Veggie-Chicken Bake

Kris Coburn, Dansville, NY

Chicken & Sausage Skilletini

I like to serve this hearty one-pan dish with French bread and olive oil for dipping.

Serves 4 to 6

1/4 c. olive oil
2 boneless, skinless chicken
  breasts, cubed
1/2 lb. spicy ground pork sausage
1 red onion, thinly sliced
2 cloves garlic, minced
14-1/2 oz. can diced tomatoes
1 red pepper, sliced
3 T. brown sugar, packed
1 t. dried basil
1/2 t. dried oregano
1/8 t. salt
1/8 t. pepper
16-oz. pkg. linguine pasta, cooked
Optional: fresh oregano leaves

Heat oil in a large skillet over medium heat. Add chicken, sausage, onion and garlic; cook until juices run clear when chicken is pierced. Add tomatoes, red pepper, brown sugar, basil, oregano, salt and pepper; simmer 5 minutes. Add cooked pasta and simmer an additional 5 minutes. Garnish with oregano, if desired.

Jen Stout, Blandon, PA

Creamy Turkey Lasagna

Use leftover turkey from family holiday feasts to make this delicious casserole.

Makes 8 servings

10-3/4 oz. can cream of mushroom
  soup
10-3/4 oz. can cream of chicken
  soup
1 c. grated Parmesan cheese
1 c. sour cream
1/4 c. chopped pimento
2 to 3 c. cooked turkey, chopped
1 c. onion, chopped
1/2 t. garlic salt
8-oz. pkg. lasagna noodles,
  cooked
2 c. shredded Cheddar cheese
Garnish: torn fresh parsley

Combine soups, Parmesan cheese, sour cream, pimento, turkey, onion and garlic salt in a large bowl; mix well. Spread one-fourth of turkey mixture on the bottom of a lightly greased 13"x9" baking pan; place several noodles on top. Alternate layers of remaining turkey and noodles; top with Cheddar cheese. Bake, uncovered, at 350 degrees for 40 to 45 minutes. Let stand 10 minutes before serving. Garnish with parsley.

Chicken & Sausage Skilletini

Sheri Fuchser, Belton, MO

Country-Time Green Beans

The secret to perfect green beans every time? Don't snap off the ends of fresh green beans until they've been cooked and cooled.

Makes 6 servings

1 lb. green beans
1 T. butter
1 T. all-purpose flour
3/4 t. sugar
1/3 c. chicken broth, warmed
3/4 t. cider vinegar
pepper to taste
3 slices bacon, crisply cooked and
    crumbled

Place green beans in a saucepan and add water to cover; bring to a boil and cook, uncovered, 2 minutes. Drain; plunge beans into cold water and drain again. Cut stems and ends off beans and set aside. Melt butter in a 12" skillet over medium heat; add flour and whisk until smooth. Combine sugar and warm broth in a small bowl, stirring until sugar dissolves; add to flour mixture and mix well. Bring to a boil; cook one minute, stirring constantly. Reduce heat; stir in vinegar and season with pepper. Add beans and bacon and cook until heated through.

★ MAKE IT EASY ★ Kitchen shears are oh-so handy for snipping fresh herbs, chopping green onions and snipping the ends off fresh green beans. Just remember to wash them with soap and water after each use.

Country-Time Green Beans

Colleen Black, Durham, NC

Summer Vegetable Salad

A "just-right" medley of color, crunch and spice!

Makes 8 servings

1 c. asparagus, cut into one-inch
   pieces
1 c. tomatoes, chopped
1 c. zucchini, shredded
1 c. red pepper, diced
2 t. balsamic vinegar
2 T. olive oil
7 dashes hot pepper sauce

Cook asparagus in a saucepan with a small amount of boiling water until crisp-tender; drain. Combine asparagus, tomatoes, zucchini and red pepper in a large bowl; toss to mix. Combine vinegar, oil and hot pepper sauce in a small bowl; whisk until well mixed. Pour dressing over salad and toss to mix.

Margaret Watson, Rochester, NY

Wild Rice Stuffing

Dates and crunchy almonds make this stuffing recipe special!

Serves 4 to 6

1-1/3 c. wild rice, uncooked
2 T. butter
2 c. onion, chopped
1 c. carrots, peeled and chopped
1 c. green pepper, chopped
6 c. herb-seasoned stuffing mix
3 c. chicken broth
10-oz. pkg. dates, chopped
1 c. slivered almonds
1/2 c. fresh parsley, chopped
1-1/2 t. dried rosemary
1-1/2 t. dried thyme
1-1/2 t. dried sage

Prepare rice according to package directions; set aside. Combine butter, onion, carrots and pepper in a medium skillet over medium-high heat and sauté until onion is tender; remove from heat. Blend in remaining ingredients; stir in rice. Spoon stuffing into a greased 3-quart casserole dish. Bake, covered, at 325 degrees for 45 minutes. Uncover and bake 15 more minutes.

Summer Vegetable Salad

Kimberly Pierotti, Milmay, NJ

Creamy Spinach Ravioli

To make this tasty dish in a snap, use ravioli and spinach in boil-in-the-bag packages. Add halved cherry tomatoes for extra color and flavor.

Makes 4 servings

25-oz. pkg. frozen cheese ravioli
2 9-oz. pkgs. frozen creamed
    spinach
salt and pepper to taste
Garnish: shaved Parmesan
    cheese

Prepare ravioli and spinach separately, according to package directions; drain. Place ravioli in a large serving bowl; top with creamed spinach and toss to coat. Add salt and pepper to taste; garnish with Parmesan cheese.

Kelli Keeton, Delaware, OH

Lasagna Rolls

When I was little, I remember standing on a chair next to my mom by the stove. I watched her roll these little bundles of noodles, meat and cheese and I would beg her to let me roll up a few. She always let me try some, and even though they were nothing compared to hers, she made me feel like they were perfect.

Makes 8 servings

1 lb. mild or sage ground pork
    sausage, cooked, crumbled and
    drained
8-oz. plus 3-oz. pkgs. cream cheese
1 bunch green onions, chopped
1 green pepper, diced
26-oz. jar spaghetti sauce, divided
16 lasagna noodles, uncooked
1-1/2 c. shredded mozzarella cheese

Combine sausage and cream cheese in the skillet where sausage was browned. Cook over low heat until cream cheese melts. Stir in onion and green pepper; remove from heat. Spread half the spaghetti sauce in the bottom of an ungreased 13"x9" baking pan; set aside. Cook lasagna noodles according to package directions; remove from heat and leave in water. Lay one noodle flat on a cutting board and spoon one to 2 tablespoons of sausage mixture at one end of the noodle. Roll the noodle and place in pan. Repeat with remaining noodles. Pour remaining sauce over top of rolls; top with mozzarella. Bake, uncovered, at 350 degrees for 15 to 20 minutes, or until cheese has melted.

Creamy Spinach Ravioli

Michelle Allman, Seymour, IN

Overnight Oriental Salad

The popular salad is always welcome at potlucks and parties!

Serves 10 to 12

3/4 c. oil
1/2 c. sugar
1/2 c. white vinegar
2 3-oz. pkgs. Oriental ramen
　 noodles with seasoning packets
1 head cabbage, shredded
1 bunch green onions, chopped
1 c. sliced almonds, toasted
1 c. roasted sunflower seeds

Combine oil, sugar, vinegar and seasoning packets from noodles in a bowl and mix well; cover and refrigerate overnight. Crush noodles in a large bowl; add cabbage, green onions, almonds and sunflower seeds. Pour oil mixture over top and toss gently.

Lynn Knepp, Montgomery, IN

Chicken-Netti

The kids will love this...It's so easy in a slow cooker.

Serves 8 to 10

16-oz. pkg. spaghetti, cooked
4 boneless, skinless chicken
　 breasts, cooked and cubed
2 c. chicken broth
10-3/4 oz. can cream of
　 mushroom soup
10-3/4 oz. can cream of chicken
　 soup
4 to 6 green onions, chopped
16-oz. pkg. pasteurized process
　 cheese spread, cubed
1/8 t. celery salt
1/8 t. pepper

Combine all ingredients in a slow cooker. Cover and cook on low setting for 2 to 3 hours, stirring frequently, until warmed through.

Overnight Oriental Salad

Kate Haney, Ellensburg, WA

Mother's Macaroni Salad

A tried & true recipe with old-fashioned flavor.

Serves 14 to 16

8 eggs, divided
1 c. cider vinegar
1 c. water
2-1/2 c. sugar
2 T. all-purpose flour
1 T. dry mustard
1 t. salt
1/2 t. celery seed
1/8 t. ground ginger
2 c. mayonnaise
2 16-oz. pkgs. elbow macaroni, cooked
1/3 c. onion, finely chopped
2 stalks celery, chopped

Hard-boil, peel and finely chop 4 eggs; set aside. Beat remaining 4 eggs in a small bowl. In a saucepan over low heat, combine vinegar, water, sugar, flour, mustard, salt, celery seed, ginger and beaten eggs. Cook and stir until boiling. Remove from heat and let cool; stir in mayonnaise. Combine cooked macaroni, hard-boiled eggs, onion and celery in a large bowl; pour vinegar mixture over all. Stir well; chill until serving time.

Sharon Crider, Lebanon, MO

Kielbasa Bean Pot

So easy to prepare...so flavorful and filling.

Serves 6 to 8

2 16-oz. cans pork & beans
1 lb. Kielbasa sausage, sliced
1-1/2 oz. pkg. onion soup mix
1/3 c. catsup
1/4 c. water
2 t. brown sugar, packed
1 T. mustard
Garnish: sliced green onions

Combine all ingredients except garnish in a 2-quart casserole dish. Bake, uncovered, at 350 degrees for one hour. Sprinkle servings with sliced green onions.

★ HANDY TIP ★ **Oversized clear glass jars make attractive canisters for storing macaroni, dried beans and rice. Because the contents are visible, you'll always know when it's time to restock.**

Mother's Macaroni Salad

Old-Fashioned Applesauce Cake, Page 190

CHAPTER FIVE

Desserts

French Apple Crisp, Page 200

Fresh Strawberry Shortcake, Page 184

Lori Simmons, Princeville, IL

Peanut Butter & Jelly Bars

If your kids like peanut butter & jelly sandwiches, they will surely love these cookie bars! Kids especially like grape jelly and strawberry jam, but you can use any flavor.

Makes 2 dozen

16-1/2 oz. tube refrigerated peanut
    butter cookie dough
1/2 c. peanut butter chips
16-oz. can buttercream frosting
1/4 c. creamy peanut butter
1/4 c. favorite jam or jelly

Let dough soften for 5 to 10 minutes at room temperature. Press dough into an ungreased 13"x9" baking pan; sprinkle with peanut butter chips. Bake at 375 degrees for 15 to 18 minutes, until lightly golden and edges are firm to the touch. Remove from oven. In a small bowl, beat together frosting and peanut butter until smooth. Spread over bars. Drop jam over frosting by teaspoonfuls. Cut through frosting with a table knife to swirl jam. Cut into bars.

Marilyn Morel, Keene, NH

Hello Dolly Bars

My sister began making these in the late 1970s. Every time I need a little pick-me-up, I make these. My sister is no longer with us, but these wonderful treats hold some very special memories for me, which I've passed down to my children and now my grandson.

Makes 12 to 16 bars

1/2 c. margarine, melted
1 c. graham cracker crumbs
1 c. sweetened flaked coconut
6-oz. pkg. semi-sweet chocolate chips
6-oz. pkg. butterscotch chips
14-oz. can sweetened condensed milk
1 c. chopped pecans

Mix together margarine and graham cracker crumbs; press into a lightly greased 9"x9" baking pan. Layer with coconut, chocolate chips and butterscotch chips. Pour condensed milk over top; sprinkle with pecans. Bake at 350 degrees for 25 to 30 minutes. Let cool; cut into bars.

★ DID YOU KNOW? ★ Evaporated milk and sweetened condensed milk were both old standbys in Grandma's day. They're still handy today, but they're not interchangeable. Condensed milk contains sugar and is cooked down to a thickened consistency, while evaporated milk contains no added sugar.

Peanut Butter & Jelly Bars

Kierstan Abrams, Los Angeles, CA

Blue-Ribbon Banana Cake

This tastes best with pecans, but feel free to substitute walnuts if you prefer.

Serves 12 to 16

1/2 c. shortening
1/4 c. plus 2 T. butter, softened and divided
2 c. sugar, divided
2 eggs
1 c. bananas, mashed
1 c. chopped pecans, divided
2 c. cake flour
1 t. baking soda
1 t. baking powder
3/4 t. salt, divided
2 t. vanilla extract, divided
1/2 c. buttermilk
1/4 c. sweetened flaked coconut
1/2 c. all-purpose flour
1/2 c. half-and-half
Garnish: sweetened flaked coconut

Combine shortening, 1/4 cup butter and 1-1/2 cups sugar in a large bowl; beat with an electric mixer at medium speed until fluffy. Add eggs and bananas; beat 2 minutes. Stir in 1/2 cup pecans. Sift together cake flour, baking soda, baking powder and 1/2 teaspoon salt; add to shortening mixture. Add one teaspoon vanilla and buttermilk; beat 2 minutes. Divide batter equally between 2 greased and floured 9" round cake pans; sprinkle batter with coconut. Bake at 350 degrees for 25 to 30 minutes. Cool layers 10 minutes before removing from pans. Combine remaining sugar, all-purpose flour, half-and-half and remaining butter in a saucepan over medium heat; cook until thickened, whisking frequently. Add remaining nuts, salt and vanilla; stirring well; cool. Place first layer, coconut-side down, on a serving platter; spread thickened sugar mixture over top. Place second layer, coconut-side up, over first cake. Swirl on Vanilla Buttercream Frosting, leaving center of cake unfrosted so coconut can be seen. Garnish with additional sweetened flaked coconut.

Vanilla Buttercream Frosting:

1 c. butter, softened
32-oz. pkg. powdered sugar
2/3 c. milk
1 T. vanilla extract

Beat butter with an electric mixer until creamy. Gradually add powdered sugar alternately with milk, beating at low speed until blended. Stir in vanilla.

Blue-Ribbon Banana Cake

Maria Jones, Tampa, FL

Cinnamon-Sugar Butter Cookies

A real old-time comfort food, good for either breakfast or dinner.

Makes 3 dozen

2-1/2 c. all-purpose flour
1/2 t. baking soda
1/4 t. salt
1 c. brown sugar, packed
1/2 c. plus 3 T. sugar, divided
1 c. butter, softened
2 eggs
2 t. vanilla extract
1 T. cinnamon

Combine flour, baking soda and salt in a bowl; mix well and set aside. Combine brown sugar and 1/2 cup sugar in a separate bowl; mix well. Add butter and beat with an electric mixer at medium speed until well blended. Add eggs and vanilla; beat 2 minutes, or until fluffy. Add flour mixture and stir just until blended. Refrigerate dough 30 minutes, or until firm. Shape dough into one-inch balls. Combine remaining sugar and cinnamon in a shallow bowl and mix well; roll balls in sugar-cinnamon mixture. Place 2 inches apart on ungreased baking sheets. Bake at 300 degrees for 18 to 20 minutes. Remove from baking sheets; cool on wire racks.

★ QUICK TIP ★ **For best results when baking cookies, allow butter and eggs to come to room temperature. Just set them out on the counter about an hour ahead of time and they'll be ready!**

Cinnamon-Sugar Butter Cookies

Tanya Leach, Adamstown, PA

Triple Fudge Cake

I get requests for this cake all the time, and nothing could be easier to make!

Makes 12 servings

3.4-oz. pkg. cook & serve chocolate pudding mix
18-1/4 oz. pkg. chocolate cake mix
12-oz. pkg. semi-sweet chocolate chips
Optional: vanilla ice cream

Prepare pudding according to package directions; stir in cake mix. Spread in a greased 13"x9" baking pan; sprinkle with chocolate chips. Bake at 350 degrees for 35 minutes; cool. Serve with vanilla ice cream, if desired.

Marilyn Epley, Stillwater, OK

Marbled Pumpkin Cheesecake

This looks so pretty on a holiday buffet table.

Serves 10 to 12

3/4 c. gingersnaps, crushed
3/4 c. graham crackers, crushed
1-1/4 c. sugar, divided
1/4 c. butter, melted
2 8-oz. pkgs. cream cheese, softened
4 eggs
15-oz. can pumpkin
1/2 t. cinnamon
1/4 t. ginger
1/4 t. nutmeg
Garnish: whipped cream, additional nutmeg

In a bowl, combine gingersnaps and graham crumbs with 1/4 cup sugar and butter. Press into the bottom of a 9" springform pan. Bake at 350 degrees for 8 to 10 minutes. In a mixing bowl, beat cream cheese until smooth. Gradually add one cup sugar; beat until light. Add eggs, one at a time, beating well after each. Transfer 1-1/2 cups of cream cheese mixture to a separate bowl and blend in pumpkin and spices. Pour half of pumpkin mixture into prepared pie crust. Top with half of cream cheese mixture. Repeat layers using remaining pumpkin and cream cheese mixtures. Using a table knife, cut through layers with uplifting motion in 4 to 5 places to create marbled effect. Bake at 325 degrees for 45 minutes without opening oven door. Turn off oven and let cake stand in oven for one hour. Remove from oven and run knife around sides of pan to remove sides. Cool and store in refrigerator. Top each serving with a dollop of whipped cream and additional nutmeg.

Triple Fudge Cake

Paige Kramer, Columbus, OH

Blueberry-Citrus Cake

I've also made this delicious cake with raspberries and blackberries.

Serves 10 to 12

18-1/4 oz. pkg. lemon cake mix
1 c. water
1/2 c. plus 2 T. orange juice, divided
1/3 c. oil
3 eggs, beaten
1-1/2 c. fresh or frozen blueberries
1 T. orange zest
1 T. lemon zest
1 c. powdered sugar
Garnish: additional orange and
   lemon zests

Beat cake mix, water, 1/2 cup orange juice, oil and eggs in a large bowl with an electric mixer at low speed for 30 seconds. Increase speed to medium; beat for 2 minutes. With a wooden spoon, gently fold in blueberries and zests. Pour batter into a greased and floured Bundt® pan. Bake at 350 degrees for 35 to 40 minutes, until a toothpick inserted in center comes out clean. Cool completely in pan on a wire rack. Remove from pan. Blend remaining orange juice and powdered sugar until smooth; drizzle over cake. Garnish with zests.

Kathy Coffman, Dallas, TX

Lone Star Pecan Cake

This rich-tasting cake needs no frosting.

Makes 16 servings

1 lb. butter, softened
2 c. sugar
6 eggs, well beaten
1 t. lemon extract
4 c. unbleached all-purpose flour
1-1/2 t. baking powder
4 c. pecan halves
2 c. golden raisins
Optional: powdered sugar

Combine butter and sugar in a large bowl. Beat with an electric mixer on medium speed until light and fluffy. Gradually add eggs and lemon extract, beating well. Sift flour and baking powder together 3 times into another large bowl; add nuts and raisins and mix well. Gradually add flour mixture to butter mixture, blending well. Spoon batter into a greased and floured 9" tube pan. Bake at 300 degrees for 1-1/2 to 2 hours, until a toothpick inserted near center comes out clean. Cool 15 minutes before removing from pan. When cool, dust with powdered sugar, if desired.

Blueberry-Citrus Cake

Holly Child, Parker, CO

Cherry-Cardamom Cookies

These sweet little bites are perfect with a cup of tea!

Makes about 3 dozen

6-oz. jar maraschino cherries, drained and diced
2-1/3 c. plus 2 T. all-purpose flour, divided
1 t. baking powder
1/2 t. baking soda
1 t. cardamom
1/2 c. butter, softened
1 c. sugar
3-oz. pkg. cream cheese, softened
1 egg
2 T. buttermilk
1 t. almond extract
Garnish: powdered sugar

Combine cherries and 2 tablespoons flour in a small bowl. Toss to mix; set aside. Combine remaining flour, baking powder, baking soda and cardamom in a medium bowl, stirring to mix. Beat butter, sugar and cream cheese in a large bowl with an electric mixer at medium speed until fluffy. Add egg, buttermilk and almond extract; beat until blended. Gradually add flour mixture to butter mixture, beating just until moistened; fold in cherry mixture. Chill for one hour. Shape dough into one-inch balls; place on ungreased baking sheets. Bake at 350 degrees for 12 to 14 minutes; remove to wire racks to cool completely. Garnish with powdered sugar. Store in an airtight container.

★ TIME SAVER ★ **No-bake sandwich cookies the children will love to make and eat! Mix one tablespoon finely chopped maraschino cherries into 1/3 cup marshmallow creme. Spread one teaspoon between 2 vanilla wafer cookies.**

Cherry-Cardamom Cookies

Kathy Zimmerman, Burley, WA

Chewy Chocolate Chip Cookies

Whenever I take these to family gatherings, everyone raves about them. My secret...use shortening rather than butter or margarine and don't bake them too long.

Makes 4 to 5 dozen

3/4 c. shortening
1 c. sugar
1 c. brown sugar, packed
2 eggs
1 t. vanilla extract
2-1/2 c. all-purpose flour
1 t. baking soda
1 t. salt
12-oz. pkg. semi-sweet chocolate
   chips
1/2 c. pecans, chopped

Combine shortening, sugar, brown sugar, eggs and vanilla in a large bowl; mix well. Add flour, baking soda and salt; mix well. Stir in chocolate chips and nuts. Drop by rounded tablespoonfuls onto ungreased baking sheets. Bake at 375 degrees for 10 to 12 minutes; do not overbake. Remove from baking sheets and cool on wire racks.

Heidi DePriest, Rancho Cucamonga, CA

Gingersnaps

We enjoy these spicy cookies for a cozy bedtime snack.

Makes about 4 dozen

3/4 c. butter, softened
1 c. sugar
1 egg
1/2 c. molasses
2 T. fresh ginger, peeled and grated
2 c. all-purpose flour
2 t. baking soda
1 t. cinnamon
1/2 t. salt
Garnish: additional sugar

Combine butter and sugar in a large bowl and blend until creamy; add egg and blend until fluffy. Add molasses and ginger; mix well and set aside. Combine flour, baking soda, cinnamon and salt in a separate bowl; mix well and add to butter mixture. Shape dough into one-inch balls. Place additional sugar in a shallow bowl; roll balls in sugar and place on lightly greased baking sheets. Bake at 350 degrees for 10 to 12 minutes; remove from baking sheets and cool on wire racks.

Chewy Chocolate Chip Cookies

Kathy Grashoff, Fort Wayne, IN

Espresso Bean Cookies

You can find chocolate-covered coffee beans in various package sizes at most coffee shops. One 6-ounce package equals about one cup.

Makes 4 dozen

1 c. butter, softened
3/4 c. brown sugar, packed
1/4 c. sugar
2 eggs
1 t. vanilla extract
2-1/4 c. all-purpose flour
1 t. baking soda
1 t. salt
1/2 t. cinnamon
1 c. chopped almonds, toasted
1 c. chocolate-covered coffee beans
4 1.4-oz. toffee candy bars, chopped

Beat butter with an electric mixer at medium speed until creamy. Gradually add sugars, beating well after each addition. Add eggs, one at a time, beating until blended after each addition; add vanilla, and beat until blended. Combine flour, baking soda, salt and cinnamon in a separate bowl. Gradually add flour mixture to butter mixture, beating well. Stir in almonds, coffee beans and chopped candy bars. Cover and chill dough until firm. Drop by teaspoonfuls onto ungreased baking sheets. Bake at 350 degrees for 10 to 11 minutes, until golden. Cool on pans one minute; remove to wire racks to cool completely. Store in an airtight container.

★ QUICK GIFT ★ Wrap several biscotti in festive cellophane and tie with curling ribbons to a package of gourmet chocolate-covered coffee beans...a coffee lover's delight!

Espresso Bean Cookies

Nancy Ramsey, Delaware, OH

Fresh Strawberry Shortcake

When time is short, use split biscuits, cubed angel food cake or waffles for a speedy version of strawberry shortcake.

Makes 8 servings

1 qt. strawberries, hulled and sliced
1 c. sugar, divided
2 c. all-purpose flour
4 t. baking powder
1/4 t. salt
1/8 t. nutmeg
1/2 c. butter
1/2 c. milk
2 eggs, separated
2 c. sweetened whipped cream

Gently toss together strawberries and 1/2 cup sugar; chill. Combine flour, 1/4 cup sugar, baking powder, salt and nutmeg in a large bowl; cut in butter with a pastry blender or fork until crumbly. Combine milk and egg yolks; mix well. Add to flour mixture, stirring just until moistened. Divide dough in half; pat into 2 greased 9" round cake pans. Beat egg whites in a small bowl at medium speed with an electric mixer until stiff peaks form; spread over dough. Sprinkle with remaining sugar. Bake at 300 degrees for 40 to 45 minutes, or until golden. Cool 10 minutes before removing from pan to a wire rack. Cool completely. Place one cake layer on a large serving plate; spread with half of whipped cream. Spoon half of strawberries over cream. Repeat layers.

★ HOMEMADE EASY ★ Top off desserts with homemade whipped cream...it's really easy to make. Whip one cup heavy cream until soft peaks form, then add one tablespoon sugar and one teaspoon vanilla extract. Continue to whip until stiff peaks form. Delicious!

Fresh Strawberry Shortcake

Rhonda Reeder, Ellicott City, MD

Gooey Toffee Scotchies

Delicious served with a dollop of whipped cream too!

Makes about 2-1/2 dozen

18-1/4 oz. pkg. yellow cake mix
1/2 c. brown sugar, packed
1/2 c. butter, melted and slightly
    cooled
2 eggs, beaten
1 c. cashews, chopped
8-oz. pkg. toffee baking bits

Beat dry cake mix, brown sugar, butter and eggs in a bowl with an electric mixer at medium speed for one minute. Stir in cashews. Press mixture into bottom of a greased 15"x10" jelly-roll pan; sprinkle with toffee bits. Bake at 350 degrees for 15 to 20 minutes, until a toothpick inserted in center comes out clean. Cool in pan and cut into bars or triangles. To serve, drizzle with warm Toffee Sauce.

Toffee Sauce:

3/4 c. plus 1 T. dark brown sugar,
    packed
2 T. dark corn syrup
6 T. butter
2/3 c. whipping cream

Bring sugar, syrup and butter to a boil in a saucepan over medium heat. Cook for 2 minutes. Carefully stir in cream and simmer for 2 more minutes, or until sauce thickens. Keep warm.

Margaret Welder, Madrid, IA

Mini Butterscotch Drop Scones

Perfect for a bake sale or church social!

Makes 3 dozen

2 c. all-purpose flour
1/2 c. brown sugar, packed
2 t. baking powder
1/4 t. salt
1/3 c. butter, softened
1 c. butterscotch chips
1/2 c. pecans, toasted and chopped
1 egg, beaten
2/3 c. whipping cream
1/2 t. vanilla extract
Optional: powdered sugar

Combine flour, brown sugar, baking powder and salt in a large bowl, stirring until blended. Cut in butter with a pastry blender or fork until crumbly. Stir in chips and nuts. Combine egg, cream and vanilla in a separate bowl, whisking until well mixed. Add egg mixture to flour mixture, stirring just until moistened. Drop by rounded tablespoonfuls onto parchment paper-lined baking sheets. Bake at 375 degrees for 12 to 15 minutes, until golden. Remove from pans and cool on wire racks. Sprinkle with powdered sugar, if desired.

Gooey Toffee Scotchies

Lynn Williams, Muncie, IN

Cool Mint Chocolate Swirls

Chocolatey cookies topped with a cool, refreshing mint wafer.

Makes 3 dozen

3/4 c. butter
1-1/2 c. brown sugar, packed
2 T. water
12-oz. pkg. semi-sweet chocolate
   chips
2 eggs
2-1/2 c. all-purpose flour
1-1/4 t. baking soda
1/2 t. salt
2 4.67-oz. pkgs. crème de menthe
   thins

Combine butter, brown sugar and water in a large saucepan; place over medium heat and cook, stirring occasionally, until butter melts and mixture is smooth. Remove from heat. Add chocolate chips, stirring until molted; cool 10 minutes. Pour chocolate mixture into a large bowl; add eggs, one at a time, stirring until well blended. Combine flour, baking soda and salt in a separate bowl, stirring to mix; add flour mixture to chocolate mixture, stirring well. Cover and chill one hour. Shape dough into walnut-size balls; place 2 inches apart on greased baking sheets. Bake at 350 degrees for 8 to 10 minutes, being careful not to overbake. Press one crème de menthe thin onto each warm cookie and let stand one minute; use back of a spoon to swirl softened thin over each cookie. Remove to wire racks to cool completely. Store in an airtight container.

★ QUICK TIP ★ When brown sugar becomes hard, simply grate the amount needed in a recipe...a quick fix!

Cool Mint Chocolate Swirls

Gail Hageman, Albion, ME

Old-Fashioned Applesauce Cake

Applesauce makes the cake moist and tender.

Serves 8 to 10

2 c. sugar
1/2 c. shortening
2 eggs
1-1/2 c. applesauce
1/2 c. water
2-1/2 c. all-purpose flour
1-1/2 t. baking soda
1-1/2 t. salt
1/4 t. baking powder
3/4 t. cinnamon
1/2 t. ground cloves
1/2 t. allspice
1/2 c. chopped walnuts
Garnish: powdered sugar,
   whipped cream, cinnamon

Beat sugar and shortening with an electric mixer at medium speed; beat in eggs, applesauce and water. Gradually add flour, baking soda, salt, baking powder and spices. Mix thoroughly; stir in nuts. Pour into a greased and floured 13"x9" baking pan. Bake at 350 degrees for one hour, or until a toothpick inserted in center comes out clean; watch that edges don't get too dark. Garnish with powdered sugar, whipped cream and cinnamon.

David Flory Columbus, OH

Pineapple-Cherry Cake

Serve with either whipped topping or ice cream.

Makes 15 servings

20-oz. can crushed pineapple
18-1/4 oz. pkg. yellow cake mix, divided
15-1/2 oz. can pitted cherries, drained
1 c. chopped walnuts or pecans
1 c. butter, melted
Optional: frozen whipped topping,
   thawed

Evenly spoon pineapple into an ungreased 13"x9" baking pan. Sprinkle half the cake mix on top; spread cherries over cake mix. Sprinkle remaining cake mix over cherries; top with nuts. Drizzle with butter. Bake at 350 degrees for 45 to 50 minutes. Garnish with whipped topping, if desired.

★ TIME SAVER ★ **Grease and flour cake pans in one easy step! Combine 1/2 cup shortening with 1/4 cup all-purpose flour. Keep this handy mix in a covered jar stored at room temperature.**

Old-Fashioned Applesauce Cake

Bunny Palmertree, Carrollton, MS

White Chocolate Cookies

Not a fan of white chocolate? Use your favorite flavor of chips instead!

Makes 5 dozen

1 c. butter, softened
3/4 c. brown sugar, packed
1/2 c. sugar
1 egg
1/2 t. almond extract
2 c. all-purpose flour
1 t. baking soda
1/4 t. cinnamon
1/4 t. ground ginger
1/4 t. salt
6-oz. pkg. white baking chocolate, chopped
1-1/2 c. chopped pecans

Beat butter and sugars in a large bowl with an electric mixer at medium speed until smooth. Add egg and extract; beat well. Combine flour, baking soda, cinnamon, ginger and salt in a separate bowl, stirring to mix; add flour mixture to butter mixture, stirring well. Blend in chocolate and pecans. Drop by teaspoonfuls 2 inches apart onto greased baking sheets. Bake at 350 degrees for 10 to 12 minutes, until lightly golden. Remove to wire racks to cool. Store in an airtight container.

Vickie, Gooseberry Patch

Raspberry Bars

Mix it up a bit by using another type of jam such as strawberry or blackberry.

Makes about 1-1/2 dozen

1 c. butter, softened
3/4 c. sugar
1 egg
1/2 t. vanilla extract
2-1/2 c. all-purpose flour
10-oz. jar seedless raspberry jam
1/2 c. chopped pecans, toasted

Beat butter and sugar in a large bowl until creamy. Add egg and vanilla, beating until blended. Add flour, beating until blended. Reserving one cup dough, press remaining dough firmly into a lightly greased 9"x9" baking pan. Spread jam evenly over crust. Stir pecans into reserved dough. Sprinkle evenly over jam layer. Bake at 350 degrees for 25 to 28 minutes, until golden. Cool completely in pan on a wire rack. Cut into bars.

White Chocolate Cookies

Barbara Girlardo, Pittsburgh, PA

Red Velvet Brownies

Who doesn't love red velvet cake?
These brownies are just wonderful!

Makes 16 servings

**4-oz. bittersweet chocolate baking
  bar, chopped**
3/4 c. butter
2 c. sugar
4 eggs
1-1/2 c. all-purpose flour
1-oz. bottle red liquid food coloring
1-1/2 t. baking powder
1 t. vanilla extract
1/8 t. salt
Optional: chopped pecans

Line bottom and sides of a
9-1/2"x9-1/2" baking pan with
aluminum foil, allowing 2 to 4 inches
to extend over sides; lightly grease
foil. Microwave chocolate and butter
in a large microwave-safe bowl on
high 1-1/2 to 2 minutes, until melted
and smooth, stirring at 30-second
intervals. Add sugar, whisking to
blend. Add eggs, one at a time,
whisking after each addition until

just blended. Gently stir in flour
and remaining ingredients except
pecans. Pour mixture into pan. Bake
at 350 degrees for 44 to 48 minutes,
until a toothpick inserted in center
comes out with a few moist crumbs.
Cool completely in pan on a wire
rack. Spread with Cream Cheese
Frosting; cut into bars. Top with
chopped pecans, if desired. Store in
refrigerator in an airtight container.

Cream Cheese Frosting:

8-oz. pkg. cream cheese, softened
3 T. butter, softened
1-1/2 c. powdered sugar
1/8 t. salt
1 t. vanilla extract

Beat cream cheese and butter in a
large bowl with an electric mixer
on medium speed until creamy.
Gradually add powdered sugar and
salt, beating until blended. Stir
in vanilla.

★ HANDY TIP ★ Need to soften cream
cheese in a hurry? Simply place an unwrapped
8-ounce block on a plate and microwave for
about a minute at 50% power.

Red Velvet Brownies

Jo Ann, Gooseberry Patch

Crunchy Fudge

Fudge is always a welcome indulgence...a great gift for friends!

Makes 3-1/3 pounds

4 c. sugar
1 c. evaporated milk
1/2 c. corn syrup
6 T. butter
1 t. vanilla extract

Combine sugar, evaporated milk, corn syrup and butter in a heavy saucepan; cook over medium-low heat until sugar dissolves. Increase heat to medium; heat to boiling, stirring occasionally. Cook without stirring, to the soft-ball stage, or 234 to 243 degrees on a candy thermometer; remove from heat. Place pan in a 1-1/2 inch deep cold water bath; add vanilla, without stirring. Let cool to 100 degrees; remove from water bath. Blend until fudge thickens and loses its gloss; spread evenly in 2 buttered 8"x8" baking pans. Pour Topping on top; cool. Cut into squares to serve.

Topping:

1 c. sugar
1/4 c. water
1/4 c. butter
2 T. evaporated milk
1 t. vanilla extract
1 c. chopped pecans, toasted

Stir sugar and water together in a small skillet; cook over medium-high heat until sugar dissolves. Increase heat to high; stir until mixture turns golden. Remove from heat; carefully add butter, evaporated milk and vanilla, stirring to mix. Add pecans; stir to coat.

Karen Adams, Cincinnati, OH

Grandma's Chocolate Fudge Cookies

Just a few ingredients make the best cookies!

Makes 5 to 6 dozen

14-oz. can sweetened condensed milk
12-oz. pkg. semi-sweet chocolate chips
1/4 c. butter
1 c. all-purpose flour
1 c. chopped nuts
1 t. vanilla extract

Place condensed milk, chocolate chips and butter in a microwave-safe bowl. Microwave, uncovered, on high, stirring every 30 seconds, until melted. Add flour, nuts and vanilla. Drop by teaspoonfuls onto greased baking sheets. Bake at 350 degrees for 7 minutes. Cool on wire racks.

Crunchy Fudge

Cora Wilfinger, Manitowoc, WI

Oma's Lemon Cheesecake

The subtle lemon flavor of this creamy dessert makes it taste light and refreshing.

Makes 12 servings

1-1/2 c. all-purpose flour
2-1/4 c. sugar, divided
1/2 c. butter, softened
4 eggs, divided
1 T. milk
2 t. vanilla extract, divided
1 t. baking powder
1/2 t. salt
2 8-oz. pkgs. cream cheese, softened
16-oz. container sour cream, divided
zest of 1 lemon, divided
Garnish: fresh lemon slices

Combine flour, 2/3 cup sugar, butter, 2 eggs, milk, one teaspoon vanilla, baking powder and salt in a large bowl; mix well. Press evenly into bottom and partially up sides of a lightly greased 9" round springform pan. For filling, beat cream cheese and 1-1/3 cups sugar with an electric mixer until smooth. Beat in remaining eggs, one at a time, beating slightly after each addition; stir in one cup sour cream, remaining vanilla and 2/3 of lemon zest. Pour cream cheese filling into crust. Bake at 325 degrees for one hour. Turn off oven; leave pan in oven for 15 minutes. For topping, mix together remaining sour cream, 1/4 cup sugar and zest until smooth. Spread sour cream topping over filling. Set oven temperature to 325 degrees. Bake at 325 degrees for 15 more minutes. Cool on wire rack for one hour. Cover and chill 8 hours. Garnish with lemon slices before serving.

★ BITE SIZE ★ **Bite-size treats always disappear fast at a potluck and are a snap to make. Simply bake a favorite cheesecake recipe in mini muffin pans.**

Oma's Lemon Cheesecake

Linda Day, Wall, NJ

French Apple Crisp

French Apple Crisp is always a favorite because it reminds me of my mother-in-law, who passed the recipe along to me.

Serves 10 to 12

1/2 c. butter, divided
4 c. apples, peeled, cored and sliced
1/4 c. rum or apple juice
2/3 c. sugar, divided
1/8 t. cinnamon
1/2 c. blanched almonds, finely chopped
1/2 c. all-purpose flour
1/8 t. salt
1/2 t. vanilla extract

Melt 1/4 cup butter in a large skillet over medium heat. Sauté apples in butter until tender, about 5 minutes. Remove from heat; pour rum or apple juice over apples. Stir in 1/3 cup sugar and cinnamon. Let stand 30 minutes. Measure almonds, flour, remaining sugar and salt into a bowl. Cut in remaining butter with pastry blender or 2 knives until mixture resembles coarse meal. Add vanilla. Evenly spread apple mixture in a greased 2-quart casserole dish or individual ramekins. Sprinkle half of the flour mixture over the apples. Bake at 400 degrees for 15 minutes. Sprinkle remaining flour mixture on top. Bake an additional 15 minutes, or until golden. Serve warm.

Sheri Dulaney, Englewood, OH

Mini Apple Hand Pies

Kids will love getting these treats as a surprise in their lunchbox.

Makes 10 servings

1 Granny Smith apple, peeled, cored and finely chopped
1/4 c. raisins
3 T. sugar
1 t. cinnamon
12-oz. tube refrigerated biscuits
2 T. butter, sliced

Combine apple, raisins, sugar and cinnamon in a bowl; toss to mix and set aside. Flatten each biscuit into a 3-inch circle. Place one tablespoon apple mixture on each biscuit; dot with butter. Bring up sides of biscuit and pinch to seal. Place in ungreased muffin cups. Bake at 375 degrees for 11 to 13 minutes, until golden.

★ TIME SAVER ★ Core apples and pears in a jiffy...cut the fruit in half, then use a melon baller to scoop out the center.

French Apple Crisp

Nichole Wrigley, Vancouver, WA

Mom & Me Peanut Butter Kisses

My mom and I first made these for the holidays...but they were so good that we make them year 'round now!

Makes about 2 dozen

1 c. creamy peanut butter
1 c. sugar
1 egg
24 milk chocolate drops, unwrapped

Combine peanut butter, sugar and egg in a bowl; mix well. Roll into small balls and arrange on an ungreased baking sheet. Bake at 350 degrees for 12 minutes. Remove from oven; immediately place a chocolate drop in the center of each cookie. Cool completely.

Lea Burwell, Charles Town, WV

White Chocolate-Cranberry Cookies

This is a family favorite...even Grandma can't resist eating one of these mouthwatering cookies!

Makes about 3-1/2 dozen

1/2 c. butter-flavored shortening
1 c. light brown sugar, packed
1/4 c. sugar
3.4-oz. pkg. instant French vanilla pudding mix
1/2 t. baking soda
1-1/2 t. vanilla extract
2-1/2 c. all-purpose flour
1-1/2 c. white chocolate chips
1 c. dried cranberries
1/2 c. macadamia nuts, crushed

Blend together shortening, sugars, dry pudding mix, baking soda, vanilla and flour in a large bowl. Fold in remaining ingredients. Drop by tablespoonfuls onto parchment paper-lined baking sheets. Bake at 375 degrees for 8 minutes.

Mom & Me Peanut Butter Kisses

Avocado Egg Sandwich, Page 216

CHAPTER SIX

Soups, Sandwiches & Snacks

Red Barn Chowder, Page 248

Rosemary Crisp Bread, Page 244

Lynda Robson, Boston, MA

Herb Garden Sandwiches

If there's any sandwich spread left over, it is delightful on a ham or roast beef sandwich instead of mayo.

Makes 16 sandwiches

2 8-oz. pkgs. cream cheese, softened
1 c. fresh herbs, finely chopped, such
    as parsley, watercress, basil,
    chervil, chives
2 t. lemon juice
1/4 t. hot pepper sauce
16 slices whole-wheat bread, crusts
    removed
paprika to taste

Combine all ingredients except bread and paprika. Spread cream cheese mixture evenly over half of bread slices. Sprinkle with paprika. Top with remaining bread slices; slice diagonally into quarters.

Kay Marone, Des Moines, IA

Iowa's Best Corn Chowder

Iowa is corn country, and this soup is a local favorite.

Makes 8 servings

1/2 c. onion, diced
1 clove garlic, minced
1/2 t. ground cumin
1 t. olive oil
4 c. vegetable broth
4 c. corn
2 new potatoes, diced
1/2 t. kosher salt
1/8 t. pepper
3/4 c. milk
1 t. fresh cilantro, chopped

Sauté onion, garlic and cumin in oil in a stockpot over medium heat for 5 minutes, or until onion is tender. Add broth and next 4 ingredients; bring to a boil. Reduce to a simmer and cook for 20 minutes, or until potatoes are tender. Add milk and cilantro; cook and stir to heat through.

★ GROW IT ★ Create a personal herb garden! Choose a narrow wooden crate that will fit on a windowsill. Fill it with starter pots of herbs...rosemary, basil, oregano and chives make a yummy kitchen sampler.

Herb Garden Sandwiches

Marisa Adams, Manchester, CT

Traditional Wedding Soup

Prepare the meatballs ahead and freeze them until you're ready to make the soup. For heartier servings, this soup is easy to double, too!

Makes 8 servings

3 qts. chicken broth
4 ripe tomatoes, peeled, seeded, chopped and juice reserved
1 head escarole, chopped
1 T. dried basil
1 T. dried parsley
pepper to taste
Garnish: fresh parsley, Parmesan cheese

In a soup pot, bring broth to a boil; add all ingredients except Meatballs and garnish. Bring to a boil. Add Meatballs, a few at a time. Bring to a boil again, reduce heat and simmer until Meatballs are cooked through, about one hour. Garnish with fresh parsley and Parmesan cheese.

Meatballs:

1 lb. ground beef
1 egg
1 clove garlic, minced
1 T. dried parsley
1/4 c. bread crumbs
1/4 c. grated Parmesan cheese

Combine all ingredients. Shape into 2-inch balls.

★ HANDY TIP ★ Dip your hands into cold water before shaping meatballs...the meat won't stick to your hands.

Traditional Wedding Soup

Lori Rosenberg, University Heights, OH

Pumpkin Seeds & Cherries Snack Mix

Always a fan favorite, especially for those who still try to eat healthy on game day!

Makes about 8 cups

3 c. pumpkin seeds
1-1/2 c. sunflower seeds
1-1/2 c. slivered almonds
1/2 c. pure maple syrup
coarse salt to taste
1-1/2 c. dried cherries or cranberries

In a large bowl, combine pumpkin seeds, sunflower seeds and almonds; toss to mix. Drizzle with syrup and stir until evenly coated. Divide mixture between 2 parchment paper-lined baking sheets, spreading evenly. Season with salt. Bake at 300 degrees for about 20 minutes, stirring several times with a wooden spoon, just until golden. Cool mixture completely on baking sheets. Add cherries or cranberries and toss to combine. Store in an airtight container at room temperature.

Lecia Stevenson, Timberville, VA

White Chocolate Party Mix

My sister Lena is always making the most delicious snacks! I ask for the recipes and they are always fast and easy. She gave me this party mix one year for a Christmas gift. I totally enjoyed it and now I make it myself.

Makes 20 cups

5 c. doughnut-shaped oat cereal
5 c. bite-size crispy corn cereal
  squares
10-oz. pkg. mini pretzel twists
2 c. salted peanuts
16-oz. pkg. candy-coated chocolates
2 12-oz. pkgs. white chocolate chips
3 T. oil

In a large heat-proof bowl, combine cereals, pretzels, peanuts and candy-coated chocolates. Toss to mix; set aside. Combine white chocolate chips and oil in a microwave-safe bowl. Microwave on medium-high for 2 minutes, stirring once. Continue to microwave on high at 30-second intervals; stir until smooth. Pour chocolate mixture over cereal mixture and stir well to coat. Spread onto 3 wax paper-lined baking sheets to cool completely. Break apart when cool. Store in an airtight container.

Pumpkin Seeds & Cherries Snack Mix

Crystal Bruns, Iliff, CO

Avocado Egg Salad Sandwiches

A fresh and delicious twist on egg salad...serve it on your favorite hearty bread!

Makes 12 sandwiches

12 eggs, hard-boiled, peeled and
   chopped
4 avocados, cubed
1 c. red onion, minced
2/3 c. mayonnaise
1/3 c. sweet pickles, chopped
2 T. mustard
salt and pepper to taste
24 slices bread

Mash eggs with a fork in a bowl until crumbly. Add remaining ingredients except bread slices. Gently mix together until blended. Spread egg mixture evenly over 12 bread slices. Top with remaining bread slices.

Lea Ann Burwell, Charles Town, WV

Ranch Chicken Wraps

My husband and my children just love these easy-to-make wraps and request them often.

Makes 8 to 10 wraps

1/2 t. oil
4 boneless, skinless chicken
   breasts, cut into strips
2.8-oz. can French-fried onions
1/4 c. bacon bits
8-oz. pkg. shredded Cheddar cheese
lettuce leaves
8 to 10 8-inch flour tortillas
Garnish: ranch salad dressing

Heat oil in a large non-stick skillet over medium heat. Add chicken; cook until chicken is golden and juices run clear when chicken is pierced. Add onions, bacon bits and cheese to skillet; cook until cheese melts. Place several lettuce leaves on each tortilla and spoon chicken mixture down center; roll up. Serve with ranch salad dressing.

★ SAVVY SECRET ★ Fresh, ripe avocados are wonderful in dips, salads and on sandwiches. To determine ripeness, gently press at the pointy end. If it gives, it's ripe! If it's still a bit firm, place in a paper bag at room temperature. Store ripe avocados in the refrigerator.

Avocado Egg Salad Sandwiches

Jo Ann, Gooseberry Patch

Red Pepper Soup

Spicy, but not too hot, it's a nice change from traditional rice soups.

Serves 12 to 14

6 red peppers, chopped
2 carrots, peeled and chopped
2 onions, chopped
1 stalk celery, chopped
4 cloves garlic, minced
1 T. olive oil
2 32-oz. containers chicken broth
1/2 c. long-grain rice, uncooked
2 t. dried thyme
1-1/2 t. salt
1/4 t. pepper
1/8 to 1/4 t. cayenne pepper
1/8 to 1/4 t. red pepper
   flakes
Garnish: croutons

In a large Dutch oven, sauté red peppers, carrots, onions, celery and garlic in olive oil until tender. Stir in broth, rice, thyme, salt, pepper and cayenne pepper; bring to a boil. Reduce heat; cover and simmer for 20 to 25 minutes, or until vegetables and rice are tender. Cool for 30 minutes. Purée in small batches in a food processor or blender, return to pan and add red pepper flakes. Heat through. Garnish with croutons.

★ HOMEMADE EASY ★ Homemade croutons add a special touch to soups and salads. Cube day-old bread, toss with olive oil and sprinkle with your favorite seasonings. Spread on a baking sheet and bake at 350 degrees for just a few minutes, until crisp.

Red Pepper Soup

Deanne Birkestrand, Minden, NE

Santa Fe Sandwiches

Add a fresh fruit salad for a quick and tasty meal with friends.

Makes 12 open-faced sandwiches

6 hoagie buns, split in half
   horizontally
1/2 c. mayonnaise
1/2 c. sour cream
1/2 t. chili powder
1/2 t. cumin
1/4 t. salt
6 tomatoes, sliced
8-oz. pkg. sliced cooked turkey
1/2 c. sliced black olives
1/3 c. green onion, sliced
3 avocados, peeled, pitted and sliced
8-oz. pkg. shredded Cheddar cheese

Arrange hoagie buns cut-side up on an ungreased baking sheet; set aside. Combine mayonnaise and next 4 ingredients; spread over hoagie buns. In the order listed, layer remaining ingredients except garnish equally on top of each bun. Bake at 350 degrees for 15 minutes. Slice each sandwich in half to serve.

Lynda Robson, Boston, MA

Slow-Cooker Sloppy Joes

Freeze any leftovers in individual servings for a quick heat & eat sandwich anytime!

Serves 14 to 18

3 c. celery, chopped
1 c. onion, chopped
1 c. catsup
1 c. barbecue sauce
1 c. water
2 T. vinegar
2 T. Worcestershire sauce
2 T. brown sugar, packed
1 t. chili powder
1 t. salt
1 t. pepper
1/2 t. garlic powder
3 to 4-lb. boneless chuck roast
14 to 18 hamburger buns, split
Optional: banana peppers, sliced
   olives, carrot crinkles, sliced
   pimentos, fresh parsley sprigs

Combine the first 12 ingredients in a 4 to 5-quart slow cooker; mix well. Add roast; cover and cook on high setting 6 to 7 hours or until tender. Remove roast; shred meat, return to slow cooker and heat through. Serve on hamburger buns. Garnish, if desired.

Santa Fe Sandwiches

Vickie, Gooseberry Patch

Black-Eyed Pea Soup

Add bacon, garlic and chiles to a classic soup recipe and you get this delicious variation! Serve with cornbread.

Serves 12 to 14

6 slices bacon, crisply cooked and
   crumbled, drippings reserved
1 onion, finely chopped
1 clove garlic, minced
1/2 t. salt
1/2 t. pepper
4-oz. can chopped green chiles,
   drained
4 15-1/2 oz. cans black-eyed peas
2 14-1/2 oz. cans beef broth
10-oz. can diced tomatoes with green
   chiles

In a Dutch oven over medium heat, cook bacon until crisp. Remove bacon, reserving drippings. Add onion, garlic, salt, pepper and chiles; sauté until onion is golden. Add bacon, undrained peas and remaining ingredients. Increase heat to medium-high and bring to a boil; remove from heat.

Beth O'Brien, Newark, DE

Chicken Stew

Let the slow cooker do all the work for you!

Serves 8 to 10

2 sweet potatoes, peeled and cubed
1 onion, sliced
6 boneless, skinless chicken breasts
1/2 t. dried thyme
1/4 t. pepper
2 bay leaves
3-1/2 c. water, divided
2 3-oz. pkgs. chicken ramen noodles
   with seasoning packets

In a 5-quart slow cooker, layer potatoes, onion and chicken. Sprinkle with thyme and pepper. Add bay leaves. Combine one cup water and seasoning packets from noodle soup, reserving noodles. Pour seasoning mixture over chicken; add remaining water to slow cooker. Cover and cook on high setting for one hour; turn to low setting and cook for 3 hours. Shred chicken. Stir in reserved noodles; increase heat to high setting and cook 10 minutes. Remove bay leaves before serving.

Black-Eyed Pea Soup

Tina Kerns, Hilliard, OH

Secret Sandwich for a Crowd

This is always a huge Buckeye game-day hit! I like to use rolled-out pizza dough from a local pizza shop instead of the frozen bread loaves for convenience.

Makes 2 sandwiches, about 18 slices per sandwich

2 16-oz. loaves frozen bread dough, thawed
1 lb. hard salami, sliced and divided
1 lb. pepperoni, sliced and divided
1-1/2 lbs. deli ham, sliced and divided
1-1/4 lbs. provolone cheese, sliced and divided
2 eggs, beaten
1 t. salt
1/2 t. dried basil

Spread one loaf of thawed dough out on a lightly greased baking sheet. Arrange slices of salami, pepperoni, ham and cheese over dough in 3 rows, using half of each ingredient. Fold over both long edges of dough toward center; pinch seams to seal. In a small bowl, whisk eggs with salt and basil; brush half of mixture lightly over top. Repeat with remaining loaf and other ingredients on a second baking sheet. Bake at 350 degrees for 30 minutes, until golden. Slice; serve warm.

★ SAVVY SECRET ★ Turn leftover bits & pieces of cheese from the fridge into a scrumptious sandwich topping. Just shred cheese and stir in enough mayo to make a spreadable consistency. Serve on crusty bread...yum!

Secret Sandwich for a Crowd

Vickie, Gooseberry Patch

Butternut Squash Soup

This is one of my favorite soups, especially in autumn!

Makes 8 servings

2-1/2 lbs. butternut squash, halved, seeded, peeled and cubed
2 c. leeks, chopped
2 Granny Smith apples, peeled, cored and diced
2 14-1/2 oz. cans chicken broth
1 c. water
seasoned salt and white pepper to taste
Garnish: freshly ground nutmeg and sour cream

Combine squash, leeks, apples, broth and water in a 4-quart slow cooker. Cover and cook on high setting for 4 hours, or until squash and leeks are tender. Carefully purée the hot soup, in 3 or 4 batches, in a food processor or blender until smooth. Add seasoned salt and white pepper. Garnish with nutmeg and sour cream.

Lisa Johnson, Hallsville, TX

Lisa's Chicken Tortilla Soup

I've tossed this soup together on many occasions. It's a snap to make... a real lifesaver when extra people turn up for supper!

Serves 6 to 8

4 14-1/2 oz. cans chicken broth
4 10-oz. cans diced tomatoes with green chiles
1 c. canned or frozen corn
30-oz. can refried beans
5 c. cooked chicken, shredded
Garnish: shredded Mexican blend cheese, corn chips or tortilla strips, chopped fresh cilantro

Combine broth and tomatoes with chiles in a large stockpot and place over medium heat. Stir in corn and beans; bring to a boil. Reduce heat to low and simmer 5 minutes, stirring frequently. Add chicken and heat through. Garnish bowls of soup as desired.

Butternut Squash Soup

Robyn Shelton, Portland, OR

Stuffed Pockets

It's so easy to make a big batch of these for a crowd, and folks just love 'em!

Makes 8 servings

6 whole pita rounds, cut in half
lettuce leaves
12 thin slices deli ham
12 slices Cheddar cheese
2 red onions, sliced into rings
2 tomatoes, sliced
ranch salad dressing to taste
8 slices bacon, crisply cooked and
    crumbled

Slightly open pita halves and stuff with lettuce, ham, cheese, onion and tomato. Top with salad dressing and crumbled bacon.

Tina Goodpasture, Meadowview, VA

Slow-Cooker Pulled Pork Sandwiches

Serve with the barbecue sauce of your choice. If hosting others, set out spicy, mild and sweet sauces so guests can choose their favorite.

Makes 12 servings

1 T. oil
3-1/2 to 4-lb. boneless pork
    shoulder roast, netted or tied
10-1/2 oz. can French onion soup
1 c. catsup
1/4 c. cider vinegar
2 T. brown sugar, packed
12 sandwich rolls, split
Garnish: sliced pickles, coleslaw

Heat oil in a skillet over medium heat. Add roast and brown on all sides; place roast in an ungreased slow cooker and set aside. Combine soup, catsup, vinegar and brown sugar in a bowl and mix well; pour over roast. Cover and cook on low setting 8 to 10 hours, until roast is fork-tender. Place roast on a platter; discard string and let stand 10 minutes. Shred roast, using 2 forks; return to slow cooker and stir to mix with sauce. Spoon meat and sauce onto rolls. Garnish with pickles and coleslaw.

Stuffed Pockets

Linda Newkirk, Central Point, OR

Minestrone Soup

My aunt gave this recipe to me about 20 years ago. It's a wonderful main dish soup and it is very easy to prepare.

Serves 6 to 8

6 slices bacon, chopped
1 onion, chopped
1 c. celery, chopped
2 cloves garlic, minced
2 t. fresh basil, chopped
1/2 t. salt
3-1/2 c. water
2 10-3/4 oz. cans bean & bacon soup
2 14-1/2 oz. cans beef broth
2 14-1/2 oz. cans stewed tomatoes, chopped and juice reserved
2 c. zucchini, peeled and chopped
2 c. cabbage, chopped
1 c. elbow macaroni, uncooked

In a large stockpot over medium heat, cook bacon, onion, celery and garlic until bacon is crisp; drain. Add remaining ingredients; bring to a boil. Reduce heat to low. Simmer until vegetables and macaroni are tender, about 15 minutes.

Krysti Hilfiger, Covington, PA

Krysti's Delicious Slow-Cooker Chili

This chili is always on hand at the Apple Cider Weekend we have in October. Made in a slow cooker... what could be easier?

Makes 6 servings

1 lb. ground beef, browned and drained
2 28-oz. cans crushed tomatoes
2 15-oz. cans light red kidney beans
3 T. dried, minced onion
1 T. chili powder
1 T. sugar or to taste
salt and pepper to taste
Garnish: shredded Cheddar cheese, chopped fresh parsley

Place all ingredients except garnish in an ungreased 4-quart slow cooker. Cover and cook on high setting 4 hours. Garnish with cheese and parsley.

★ HOT TIP ★ Jazz up biscuits to serve alongside your favorite soup or chili. Just dip frozen biscuits in melted butter and a mixture of Parmesan cheese, minced garlic and a little dried rosemary, then bake as directed.

Minestrone Soup

Tanya Graham, Lawrenceville, GA

Chili with Corn Dumplings

Dumplings created with cornmeal and fresh cilantro make this chili extra special and so satisfying.

Makes 10 servings

4-1/2 lbs. ground beef
2-1/4 c. onion, chopped
3 15-oz. cans corn, divided
3 14-1/2 oz. cans stewed tomatoes
3 15-oz. cans tomato sauce
1 T. hot pepper sauce
6 T. chili powder
1 T. garlic, minced
1-1/3 c. biscuit baking mix
2/3 c. cornmeal
2/3 c. milk
3 T. fresh cilantro, chopped

Brown ground beef and onion in a Dutch oven over medium heat; drain. Set aside 1-1/2 cups corn; stir remaining corn with liquid, tomatoes, sauces, chili powder and garlic into beef mixture. Bring to a boil. Reduce heat; cover and simmer 15 minutes. Combine baking mix and cornmeal in a medium bowl; stir in milk, cilantro and reserved corn just until moistened. Drop dough by rounded tablespoonfuls onto simmering chili. Cook over low heat, uncovered, 15 minutes. Cover and cook 15 to 18 more minutes or until dumplings are dry on top.

★ FREEZE IT ★ Freeze leftover chili in small containers...later, pop in the microwave for chili dogs, nachos or baked potatoes at a moment's notice. A terrific time-saver!

Chili with Corn Dumplings

Julie Horn, Chrisney, IN

Texas Steak Sandwiches

We like provolone, but use whatever kind of cheese your family likes best.

Makes 8 open-faced sandwiches

8 slices frozen Texas toast
1-1/2 lbs. deli roast beef, sliced
 steak sauce to taste
16 slices provolone cheese
Optional: sautéed green pepper
 and red onion slices

Place Texas toast on an ungreased baking sheet. Bake at 425 degrees for 5 minutes per side, or until softened and lightly golden; set aside. Warm roast beef in a skillet over medium heat until most of juice has evaporated; stir in steak sauce. Place one cheese slice on each toast slice. Divide beef evenly among toast slices; top with remaining 8 cheese slices and, if desired, sautéed green pepper and onion slices. Place beef-topped toast on an ungreased baking sheet; bake at 425 degrees until cheese melts.

Arden Regnier, East Moriches, NY

Spicy Squash Soup

One year we were getting tired of eating leftover Thanksgiving turkey, and I had a lot of leftover squash too. So I came up with this recipe...it's a satisfying supper with a basket of cornbread muffins.

Serves 6 to 8

2 butternut squash, peeled, seeded
 and cubed
1 stalk celery, finely diced
1 jalapeño pepper, seeded and finely
 diced
1/2 onion, finely diced
2 c. chicken broth
12-oz. can evaporated milk
1/2 c. brown sugar, packed
1/2 c. water
salt and pepper to taste
ground cumin to taste

Place squash in a large saucepan and cover with water. Cook over medium-high heat until tender; drain. Mash squash and measure out 4 cups. Return 4 cups squash to saucepan over medium-low heat; stir in remaining ingredients except cumin. Simmer, covered, for 45 minutes. Cool slightly. Purée soup until smooth, adding to a blender in small batches. Return soup to saucepan over low heat just long enough to heat through; stir in cumin.

Texas Steak Sandwiches

Dan Ferren, Terre Haute, IN

Dan's Broccoli & Cheese Soup

My boss used to make an amazing broccoli & cheese soup. Now that I'm a stay-at-home dad, I tried to recreate it...I think my version is better than the original!

Makes 6 servings

16-oz. pkg. frozen chopped
   broccoli, thawed
10-3/4 oz. can cream of
   mushroom soup
1 c. milk
1 c. half-and-half
8-oz. pkg. cream cheese, cubed
1-1/2 c. pasteurized process cheese
   spread, cubed
garlic powder and pepper to taste

Combine all ingredients in an ungreased slow cooker; cover and cook on high setting 30 to 40 minutes. Reduce setting to low; cook an additional 3 to 4 hours, stirring occasionally.

Sabrina Collins, Huron, OH

Extra-Cheesy Grilled Cheese

Delicious in winter with a steaming bowl of tomato soup...scrumptious in summer made with produce fresh from the garden!

Makes 4 sandwiches

1/4 c. butter, softened
8 slices sourdough bread
4 slices provolone cheese
4 slices mozzarella cheese
Optional: 4 slices red onion,
   4 slices tomato, 1/4 c. chopped
   fresh basil

Spread 1-1/2 teaspoons butter on each of 8 bread slices. Place one bread slice, butter-side down, in a large skillet or on a hot griddle. Layer one slice provolone and one slice mozzarella cheese on bread slice. Top with an onion slice, tomato slice and one tablespoon basil, if desired. Top with a bread slice butter-side up. Reduce heat to medium-low. Cook until golden on one side, about 3 to 5 minutes; flip and cook until golden on other side. Repeat to cook remaining sandwiches.

Dan's Broccoli & Cheese Soup

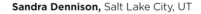

Shawna Weathers, Judsonia, AR

Dressed-Up Dogs

My mother used to fix hot dogs this way when I was a child and now my own children are happy when I do it.

Makes 4 sandwiches

8 hot dogs
8 slices rye bread, toasted
mayonnaise-type salad dressing
 to taste
2 kosher dill pickles, each cut
 lengthwise into 4 slices
4 slices Swiss cheese
Optional: mustard to taste

Slice hot dogs lengthwise, taking care not to cut all the way through. Place hot dogs cut-side down on a lightly greased hot griddle. Cook on each side until golden and heated through; set aside. Spread 4 slices bread with salad dressing; top each with 2 pickle slices, 2 hot dogs and one slice cheese. Spread remaining 4 slices bread with mustard, if using. Place on top of sandwiches.

Sandra Dennison, Salt Lake City, UT

Easy Tomato Soup

Other tasty additions to try...chopped fresh basil, chopped fresh chives, chopped fresh rosemary, croutons, freshly grated Parmesan cheese and grated lemon zest.

Makes 11 cups

28-oz. can Italian-seasoned diced
 tomatoes
26-oz. can tomato soup
32-oz. container chicken broth
1/2 t. pepper
Optional: sour cream, chopped
 fresh basil

Pulse tomatoes with juice in a food processor or blender 3 to 4 times, or until finely diced. Stir together tomatoes, soup, chicken broth and pepper in a Dutch oven. Cook over medium heat, stirring occasionally, for 10 minutes, or until thoroughly heated. Top servings with sour cream and chopped fresh basil, if desired.

★ BITE SIZE ★ Try something new... grilled cheese croutons! Make grilled cheese sandwiches as usual, then slice them into small squares. Toss into a bowl of creamy tomato soup...yum!

Dressed-Up Dogs

Debi DeVore, Dover, OH

Herb Garden Bread

Enjoy this braided bread warm
from the oven with butter.

Makes one loaf

3 to 4 c. all-purpose flour, divided
3 T. sugar
2 envs. active dry yeast
1-1/2 t. salt
1/4 t. dried marjoram
1/4 t. dried thyme
1/2 c. water
1/4 c. milk
1/4 c. butter, sliced
1 egg
1 T. butter, melted

Combine 1-1/2 cups flour, sugar, yeast, salt, marjoram and thyme in a large bowl; mix well. Combine water, milk and butter in a small saucepan over medium heat. Heat until very warm, about 120 to 130 degrees; add to flour mixture and mix well. Add egg and enough of the remaining flour to make a soft dough. Turn dough out onto a lightly floured surface and knead 5 minutes, adding more flour if needed to prevent dough from sticking. Place dough in a lightly greased bowl; turn to coat top. Cover and let rise until double in bulk. Punch down dough and place on a lightly floured surface. Separate dough into 3 sections and let stand 10 minutes. Roll each section into a 30-inch rope; braid the 3 ropes together and form into a circle, pinching ends together to seal. Place on a lightly greased baking sheet; cover and let rise until double in bulk. Bake at 375 degrees for 30 minutes, covering with aluminum foil if necessary to prevent browning. Brush with melted butter and cool before slicing.

★ SHAKE IT ★ Use dried herbs from the herb garden to make a terrific seasoning blend. Combine one cup sea salt with 2 tablespoons each of rosemary, thyme, lemon balm, mint, tarragon, dill weed and paprika. Stir in 4 tablespoons parsley and basil. Blend, in batches, in a food processor, and store in a glass shaker.

Herb Garden Bread

Karen Pilcher, Burleson, TX

The Ultimate Shrimp Sandwich

Treat your family and friends to this scrumptious recipe.

Makes 6 sandwiches

3/4 lb. cooked shrimp, peeled and chopped
1/4 c. green pepper, chopped
1/4 c. celery, chopped
1/4 c. cucumber, chopped
1/4 c. tomato, diced
1/4 c. green onions, chopped
1/4 c. mayonnaise
Optional: hot pepper sauce to taste
6 split-top rolls, split and lightly toasted
2 T. butter, softened
1 c. shredded lettuce

Combine shrimp, vegetables, mayonnaise and hot pepper sauce, if using, in a large bowl; toss well and set aside. Spread rolls evenly with butter; divide lettuce among rolls and top with shrimp mixture.

Jennifer Licon-Conner, Gooseberry Patch

Ultimate Nachos

This crowd-pleaser is loaded with ooey-gooey cheese and all your favorite toppings.

Serves 6 to 8

1/3 c. onion, finely chopped
1 clove garlic, minced
1 T. olive oil
16-oz. can refried beans
1/2 c. salsa
13-oz. pkg. restaurant-style tortilla chips
1-1/2 c. shredded Monterey Jack cheese
1-1/2 c. shredded Cheddar cheese
pickled jalapeño slices, well drained
Optional: 1 c. guacamole, 1/2 c. sour cream
Optional: chopped fresh cilantro, sliced ripe olives, shredded lettuce, additional salsa

In a skillet over medium heat, sauté onion and garlic in oil for 4 to 5 minutes, until onion is tender. Add beans and salsa to skillet, stirring until beans are creamy. Cook one minute or until heated through. Scatter most of chips on a parchment paper-lined large baking sheet or an oven-proof platter. Top with bean mixture, cheeses and desired amount of jalapeños. Bake at 450 degrees for 8 minutes or until cheeses melt and edges are golden. Garnish with small dollops of guacamole and sour cream, if desired. Garnish with cilantro, olives, lettuce and salsa, if desired. Serve hot.

The Ultimate Shrimp Sandwich

Sharon Tillman, Hampton, VA

Rosemary Crisp Bread

Try cutting this bread into sticks or cubes to dunk in warm soup.

Makes 10 servings

11-oz. tube refrigerated pizza
   crust dough
2 T. Dijon mustard
1 T. garlic, minced
2 t. olive oil
1-1/2 c. shredded Cheddar &
   mozzarella pizza-blend cheese
1 t. dried rosemary

Unroll pizza crust dough on a lightly greased jelly-roll pan; pat out dough to a 12-inch by 10-inch rectangle. Bake at 425 degrees for 5 minutes. Combine mustard, garlic and oil in a small bowl and mix well; spread evenly over baked crust. Sprinkle with cheese and rosemary. Bake 12 to 15 more minutes, until cheese melts and crust is crisp and golden.

Deanne Birkestrand, Minden, NE

The Best-Yet Buffalo Wings

These wings are sweet, but the sauce is hot!

Makes about 3 dozen

3 lbs. chicken wings
seasoned salt to taste
2-oz. bottle hot pepper sauce
1 c. brown sugar, packed
1 c. water
1 T. mustard seed

Arrange chicken wings on a lightly greased 15"x10" jelly-roll pan. Sprinkle with seasoned salt. Bake at 400 degrees for 20 minutes; turn wings. Bake for 20 to 30 more minutes, until golden and juices run clear when chicken is pierced with a fork; drain. Arrange on serving platter. Combine remaining ingredients in a saucepan; bring to a boil over medium heat. Reduce heat to low; cook until mixture caramelizes and becomes a dark burgundy color, stirring occasionally. Pour sauce over wings before serving or serve on the side for dipping.

Rosemary Crisp Bread

Kathryn Harris, Lufkin, TX

Fiesta Cornbread

If you'd like, shred Pepper Jack cheese and substitute for the Cheddar...it will add more kick!

Serves 6 to 9

1 c. cornmeal
1 c. buttermilk
8-oz. can creamed corn
2 jalapeño peppers, chopped
1/2 t. salt
3/4 t. baking soda
2 eggs, beaten
1 onion, chopped
1/4 c. oil
1 c. shredded Cheddar cheese,
    divided

Combine first 8 ingredients; set aside. Heat oil in an 8" to 10" cast-iron skillet; pour in half the batter. Sprinkle with half the cheese; pour remaining batter over top. Sprinkle with remaining cheese. Bake at 400 degrees for 30 minutes.

Donna Carter, Knoxville, TN

Christmas Tree Pull-Apart Rolls

Very yummy...so festive with dinner!

Makes 3 dozen

48-oz. pkg. (36 count) frozen rolls
2 T. butter, melted
2 t. dried parsley, crumbled
garlic salt to taste
1/4 c. grated Romano cheese
additional dried parsley to taste

Arrange rolls on a baking sheet in a Christmas tree pattern. (As they rise, the "balls" come together.) Bake according to package directions. When you remove them from the oven, they will be formed into a single piece. Transfer to a platter. Combine butter, parsley and garlic salt; brush onto rolls. Sprinkle with cheese and dried parsley. Serve immediately.

★ BUTTER IT UP ★ When serving rolls alongside main dishes, dress up 1/2 cup of butter by softening it, then blending in 2 teaspoons orange zest. Place butter on a sheet of wax paper and roll into a log shape. Chill for 2 to 3 hours until firm. Store any leftovers in the refrigerator.

Fiesta Cornbread

Suzanne Pottker, Elgin, IL

Red Barn Chowder

Enjoy the spicy taste of this delicious, hearty chowder filled with sausage and vegetables.

Serves 8 to 10

1 lb. ground hot Italian pork sausage, crumbled
1 onion, chopped
3 stalks celery, chopped
1 green pepper, chopped
1 red pepper, chopped
2 zucchini, quartered and sliced
3 to 4 cloves garlic, chopped
28-oz. can stewed tomatoes
10-oz. can diced tomatoes with green chiles
6-oz. can tomato paste
1 c. water
2 t. dried basil
salt and pepper to taste
1 c. canned garbanzo beans, drained and rinsed

Combine sausage, onion, celery, peppers, zucchini and garlic in a large saucepan. Sauté until sausage is browned and vegetables are tender; drain. Stir in tomatoes with juice, tomato paste, water, basil, salt and pepper; cook until heated through. Add garbanzo beans; heat through.

Gen Mazzitelli, Binghamton, NY

Cheesy Garlic Bread

I love to serve this yummy bread with my homemade beef stew... it's a "must" alongside any favorite pasta dish too.

Makes 12 servings

1/4 c. canola oil
2 T. fresh parsley, minced
1 T. garlic, minced
1/2 t. salt
1/4 t. pepper
1 loaf French or Italian bread, halved lengthwise
grated Parmesan cheese to taste

Combine oil, parsley, garlic, salt and pepper in a small bowl; mix well and spread over bread halves. Place bread halves on a lightly greased baking sheet. Bake at 400 degrees for 5 to 8 minutes, until golden. Immediately sprinkle generously with cheese. Cut each bread half into 6 slices.

★ PARTY PERFECT ★ When serving soups and stews for a get-together, stack 2 or 3 cake stands, then fill each tier with a different type of roll, biscuit or bread for guests to try.

Red Barn Chowder

Kay Marone, Des Moines, IA

Corn Dogs

Fun to serve at a backyard picnic!

Serves 8 to 10

1 c. all-purpose flour
2 T. sugar
1-1/2 t. baking powder
1 t. salt
2/3 c. cornmeal
2 T. shortening
1 egg
3/4 c. milk
8 to 10 hot dogs
8 to 10 wooden sticks
oil for deep frying

Combine flour, sugar, baking powder and salt; stir in cornmeal. Using a pastry cutter or 2 forks, cut in shortening until coarse crumbs form; set aside. Blend together egg and milk in a separate bowl. Stir into flour mixture. Thoroughly dry each hot dog with a paper towel to ensure batter will cling. Insert a stick into each; dip in mixture. Deep-fry in 350 to 375-degree oil 4 to 5 minutes or until golden.

Nancy Wise, Little Rock, AR

Hula Ham Wraps

Try these with deli turkey slices too!

Makes 12 wraps

3/4 lb. deli ham, sliced into strips
20-oz. can pineapple tidbits, drained
2 carrots, peeled and shredded
1 head napa cabbage, shredded
1 c. sour cream
1/4 c. white wine vinegar
1 t. salt
1/4 t. pepper
Optional: 1 t. caraway seed
12 10-inch flour tortillas

Combine ham, pineapple, carrots and cabbage in a large bowl; set aside. In a separate bowl, whisk together sour cream, vinegar, salt, pepper and caraway seed, if desired. Pour over ham mixture; toss. Divide among tortillas and roll into wraps.

★ SAVVY SWAP ★ If time is short, use bagged shredded cabbage for coleslaws and salads.

Corn Dogs

Cookies, Bars & Brownies

Desserts

Dips & Spreads

U. S. to Metric Recipe Equivalents

Volume Measurements

¼ teaspoon .... 1 mL
½ teaspoon .... 2 mL
1 teaspoon .... 5 mL
1 tablespoon = 3 teaspoons.......... 15 mL
2 tablespoons = 1 fluid ounce....... 30 mL
¼ cup................................ 60 mL
⅓ cup................................ 75 mL
½ cup = 4 fluid ounces.............. 125 mL
1 cup = 8 fluid ounces.............. 250 mL
2 cups = 1 pint = 16 fluid ounces .. 500 mL
4 cups = 1 quart........................ 1 L

Weights

1 ounce............................... 30 g
4 ounces............................. 120 g
8 ounces............................. 225 g
16 ounces = 1 pound.................. 450 g

Baking Pan Sizes

Square
8x8x2 inches............ 2 L = 20x20x5 cm
9x9x2 inches.......... 2.5 L = 23x23x5 cm

Rectangular
13x9x2 inches.......... 3.5 L = 33x23x5 cm

Loaf
9x5x3 inches............. 2 L = 23x13x7 cm

Round
8x1-1/2 inches............. 1.2 L = 20x4 cm
9x1-1/2 inches............. 1.5 L = 23x4 cm

Recipe Abbreviations

t. = teaspoon   ltr. = liter
T. = tablespoon   oz. = ounce
c. = cup   lb. = pound
pt. = pint   doz. = dozen
qt. = quart   pkg. = package
gal. = gallon   env. = envelope

Oven Temperatures

300˚ F .... 150° C
325˚ F............................. 160° C
350˚ F............................. 180° C
375˚ F............................. 190° C
400˚ F .... 200° C
450˚ F............................. 230° C

Kitchen Measurements

A pinch = ⅛ tablespoon
1 fluid ounce = 2 tablespoons
3 teaspoons = 1 tablespoon
4 fluid ounces = ½ cup
2 tablespoons = ⅛ cup
8 fluid ounces = 1 cup
4 tablespoons = ¼ cup
16 fluid ounces = 1 pint
8 tablespoons = ½ cup
32 fluid ounces = 1 quart
16 tablespoons = 1 cup
16 ounces net weight = 1 pound
2 cups = 1 pint
4 cups = 1 quart
4 quarts = 1 gallon